I Wanna Be Sedated

30 Writers on Parenting Teenagers

Edited by
Faith Conlon and Gail Hudson

SEAL PRESS

Published by Seal Press
An Imprint of Avalon Publishing Group, Incorporated
1400 65th Street, Suite 250
AVALON
publishing group incorporated Emeryville, CA 94608

ISBN 1-58005-127-8

Library of Congress Cataloging-in-Publication Data
I wanna be sedated: 30 writers on parenting teenagers /
edited by Faith Conlon and Gail Hudson.
p. cm.
ISBN 1-58005-127-8
1. Parent and teenager. 2. Teenagers—Family relationships. 3. Parenting. I. Conlon, Faith, 1955- II. Hudson, Gail E.
HQ799.15.I14 2005
306.874—DC22
2004030251

9 8 7 6 5 4 3 2 1

Cover and interior design: Gia Giasullo, Studio eg
Printed in the United States of America by Malloy
Distributed by Publishers Group West

For Gabrielle and Tennessee
and
Erin, Scott, and Connor

CONTENTS

TELL IT LIKE IT IS

PIECE OF MY HEART

Introduction

WE MET IN A PLACE where mothers have met for generations: in the hallway of the local elementary school. In between chasing down lost jackets and errant homework assignments, we discovered that we were both professionally involved in writing and editing. Before long, one of us had roped the other into co-leading an after-school writer's club, and we began taking long walks through our Seattle neighborhood, brainstorming writing exercises for our students and getting better acquainted.

As mothers tend to do, we often talked about our children. While the friendship deepened, so did the conversations about parenting. Gail confided that she was struggling with her then-sixteen-year-old daughter's curfew breaking and other routine acts of teenage rebellion. Faith, who had the fortune of being a stepmom to two children, now in their twenties, offered Gail "been-there" advice as well as a unique perspective, one that might be called parental love without the psychosis. Through the sharing of stories, we discovered that our frustration or weariness would often shift into thoughtful insight, or dissolve into gales of laughter. On good walks, we'd have a little of both.

After we had walked and talked through several seasons and parenting crises, an idea for a book project began taking shape. Why not create a collection of personal essays that would illuminate this unique phase of parenting? If we found such pleasure in swapping stories about our intense love and irrational anger while parenting teens, maybe others would, too. Certainly we had many friends in the same boat, adrift in the roiling seas of adolescent behavior, waiting for the search-and-rescue team to arrive. Perhaps we could create a kind of life raft for parents of teens—something to grab on to when you need support or guidance or just a good laugh.

We weren't "experts," however, and we didn't want to write a book of advice. What we came to realize is that parents of all ages, but especially of teenagers, hunger for the honesty of true stories. So often, parenting books offer advice that is hard to plug into the messiness of real life. What we really want to hear is how another parent handled a daughter's budding sexuality, a son's sudden slacker attitude toward school, or the shocking discovery that your teenager actually lies. We want to know that we're not crazy, that we are not alone, and that other parents are stumbling and fumbling, too. Stories build community—and parents of teenagers especially need and crave a community.

From the outset, we decided that we would turn to writers to tell the stories parents want to hear. As a culture, we rely on storytellers to be our collective mirror, to bring truth and perspective to life. Knowing this, we approached seasoned essayists, journalists, memoirists, and novelists who have thoughtfully chronicled the truths of parenthood in their work.

We also put out a general call for submissions and were immediately flooded with hundreds of essays. Clearly we had struck a chord, perhaps with our tongue-in-cheek title for the anthology. It was inspired by a Ramones song from the punk era of the 1970s—well before our teenagers were born—but it also evoked the feelings parents sometimes have in the face of adolescent rebellion.

We had fun playing with the title, but didn't actually intend for it to become permanent. After all, most of us want to be awake and engaged with our teens. Yet, we couldn't help noticing that everyone laughed when they heard the title, and we couldn't exactly call the book "I Wanna Communicate with You." The title stuck.

As it turned out, finding a title was much easier than choosing from all the submissions we received. We were struck by the depth of feeling this topic inspired, and the real-life stories ran the gamut from hilarious to heartbreaking. Some were selected because they spoke specifically to a mother's experience, such as the madness of menopausal mood swings—or a dad's, with one father reluctantly venturing into Boy Scouts. Some we liked because they had a kitchen-table intimacy to them: one parent speaking frankly to another. Some we chose simply because they made us laugh out loud.

Ultimately, it was our contributors who helped us discover the shape of the book, starting with the first section, where we explore what it feels like to have sons and daughters on the cusp of adolescence. From there we move into the nitty-gritty of parenting teens, including the age-old fretters—sex, drugs, rock 'n' roll, and will this kid ever get into college? Like a conversation between friends, as we go deeper into the book, the topics tend to get meatier—the entrenched racism faced by black male teens, a teenage girl struggling with body image, and what happens when your child finds the call of the streets stronger than the call of home.

Initially, we were surprised that we didn't receive more essays about the harder issues that many teens grapple with: substance abuse, depression, eating disorders, gender identity. Did we not do enough to invite these conversations? Of course, we'll never really know the answer. But in the end, we came to believe that the reason so few writers chose to explore the more sensitive zones was simply because parents wanted to protect their children's privacy. Writing an essay about the concerns of early childhood—a colicky infant, a toddler who bites—doesn't seem nearly as invasive as revealing the details of a son's suicidal depression or the torture of a daughter's anorexia.

The courageous contributors who did delve into the tough material struck the right tone, revealing more about themselves and the vulnerability of parenting than trying to interpret the teen's experience. Even so, parental insights often come only with the passage of time, written after the children are grown. When hard times happen during adolescence, it is a painful place in family history, and even the distance of years gone by doesn't always make it safe to open it up for public scrutiny. Knowing which stories belong to the parents and which stories the child rightfully owns seems a fitting metaphor for the separation process between parent and teen.

The essays that appear in this anthology don't necessarily reflect our own approaches to parenting. Instead, each reveals a writer who thought hard, loved deeply, and was willing to share some truth, some hard-earned lesson, or at least be generous enough to let us laugh at his or her predicament. How these parents faced different situations—a daughter's tattoo, a son's fascination with Marilyn Manson, another's experimentation with drugs—sparked many conversations between us. What would we have done in that situation? Would we have reacted as strongly, stayed as calm? Our hope is that these essays will provoke similar conversations and insights for our readers.

As we read through the stacks of submissions, we were also inspired by how much parents admire their teenagers, and how often this appreciation is reciprocated. Perhaps this should come as no surprise. According to a recent survey titled "State of Our Nation's Youth," 50 percent of the high school students surveyed say they would like to spend more time with their families, and almost 75 percent say they get along with their parents or guardians "very well, if not extremely well." Still, it is inevitable that teenagers battle with their parents, if only to forge their own identities. Given the close relationship we have with our teenagers—with many of us sharing similar tastes in music, movies, and clothes—our common parent-teen struggles can be bewildering and painful for both generations.

Even so, the parents we heard from understand and respect their teens' need to stretch and grow. Many writers addressed the small, humble moments of connection, and the bittersweet difficulty of watching our young ones grow up and then grow away. If there is any phase of life more poignant than our own coming of age, it is guiding our children through this enormous transition. The final section of the book pays tribute to the deep emotions this task engenders: the yearning to hold on, and the mandate to let go.

Although this book is a freeze-frame of adolescence—with each writer capturing a particular moment in a particular household—we are also reminded that the raising of teenagers is just one phase in a parent's lifetime. Few of us skated through our own adolescence without moments of angst, self-doubt, or confusion. If we can look back on our youth with the humor and wisdom we now have, surely we'll eventually gain the same perspective on these years of parenting teenagers. In the words of one of our generation's heroes, George Harrison, "All things must pass."

But for now, here we are in the throes of it. One week we're sure that everything can be fixed with an extra-large pizza or extra-long dorm-room sheets, the next week we are absolutely powerless to make our child feel better during a rough stretch. We hope these stories offer comfort and camaraderie for the days when you are muddling through, and inspiration for the days when you need it most.

Faith Conlon and Gail Hudson
January 2005

Too Late to Turn Back Now

Teenager Owner's Manual

W. Bruce Cameron

CONGRATULATIONS! You are now the proud new owner of a teenage daughter. Please read this manual carefully, as it describes the maintenance of your new daughter and answers important questions about your warranty (which does NOT include the right to return the product to the factory for a full refund).

IF YOU FEEL YOU HAVE RECEIVED YOUR TEENAGER IN ERROR:

To determine whether you were supposed to receive a teenage girl, please examine your new daughter carefully. Does she (a) look very similar to your original daughter, only with more makeup and less clothing? (b) refuse to acknowledge your existence on the planet Earth (except when requesting money)? (c) sleep in a burrow of dirty laundry? If any of these are true, you have received the correct item. Nice try, though.

BREAK-IN PERIOD:

When you first receive your teenage daughter, you will experience a high level of discomfort. Gradually, this discomfort will subside and you will merely feel traumatized. This is the "Break-In Period," during which you will become accustomed to certain behaviors that will cause you concern, anxiety, and stress. Once you have adapted to these behaviors, your teenager will start acting even worse.

ACTIVATION:

To activate your teenage daughter, simply place her in the vicinity of a telephone. No further programming is required.

SHUTDOWN:

Several hours after activation, you may desire to shut down your teenage daughter. There is no way to do this.

CLEANING YOUR TEENAGE DAUGHTER:

Having a teenage daughter means learning the difference between the words "clean" and "neat." Teenage daughters are very clean because they take frequent showers that last more than an hour. They will scrub themselves with expensive, fragrant soaps, which you must purchase for them because like I'm *sure* I'm going to use like the same kind of soap my mom and dad use. When they have completely drained the hot-water tank, they will step out and wrap themselves in every towel in the bathroom, which they will subsequently strew throughout the house. If you ask them to pick up the towels, you are confusing "clean" with "neat." Teenagers are very busy and do not have time to be neat. They expect others to pick up after them. These others are called "parents."

FEEDING YOUR TEENAGE DAUGHTER:

Your teenage daughter requires regular meals, which must be purchased for her at restaurants because she detests everything *you* eat because it is, like, so disgusting. She does not want you to accompany her to these restaurants because some people might see you and like I'm sure I want my friends to see me eating dinner with my *parents*. Either order take-out food or just give her the money, preferably both. If you order pizza, never answer the doorbell because the delivery boy might see you and ohmigod he is so hot. Yes, your daughter's idea of an attractive man is the *pizza boy*.

CLOTHING YOUR TEENAGE DAUGHTER:

Retailers make millions of dollars a year selling stylish and frankly sensible clothing that will look adorable on your daughter. If you enjoy shopping, you will love the vast selections that are available. Unfortunately, your teenage daughter wants to dress like a lap dancer. You may be able to coerce her into putting on a cute outfit before leaving the house, but by the time she walks in the schoolhouse door, she will be wearing something entirely different.

OTHER MAINTENANCE:

Teenage daughters require one of two levels of maintenance: "High" and "Ultra High." Your daughter is "Ultra High." This means that whatever you do won't be enough and whatever you try won't work.

WARRANTY:

This product is not without defect because she has your genes, for heaven's sake. If you think this is not fair, talk to your parents, who think it is hilarious. Your teenage daughter will remain a teenager for as long as it takes for her to become a woman, which in her opinion has already happened and as far as you are concerned never really will. If you are dissatisfied with your teenage daughter, well, what did you expect? In any event, your warranty does not give you your little girl back under any circumstances, except that deep down, she's actually still there—you just have to look for her.

Shopping for Kotex

Jeffrey K. Wallace

ONCE A YEAR, my wife leaves town without me. She flies to Denver to visit her sister. They get together to climb mountains, count calories, and talk about how independent their mother was. I get to stay home with the kids.

I welcome these little breaks. I get to go to bed alone and turn up the TV as loud as I want, and I make lots of jokes about throwing big, messy parties with live music and strangers in our living room. I wouldn't actually do that kind of thing, of course—not with the kids around, never in this neighborhood—but I wouldn't mind knowing a few guys who would.

When I dropped Katherine off at the airport, she gave me a squeeze and kissed me with her eyes wide open, right there on the sidewalk, by the baggage handlers. And I knew by the look in her eye that she was warning me: If I screw this family up while she's out of town, I'm toast.

"See you in a few days," she said with a final peck.

The kids waved and Katherine waved back and we stood around blowing kisses as she picked up her little bag and disappeared into the terminal. I immediately jumped into the driver's seat. "Party time!" I called out, over screeching tires. "Who wants Baskin-Robbins?"

WE SURVIVED THE FIRST couple days as we always do without her—on macaroni and microwavables. My five-year-old son didn't complain, but his sister, Sarah—my eleven-year-old—had homemade expectations. Sarah's a lot like her mom: a quietly confident girl who gets straight A's and has a million friends. She's also blond, blue-eyed, and tall—already a good six inches taller than her fifth-grade teacher. We never tell her she's big, but everyone else does.

On our third night alone, we ate pizza and I insisted the kids watch a part of *A Hard Day's Night* with me. I told them about how the Beatles came to my house when I was kid, but they weren't impressed. The only thing that impressed my son was the idea that one of those guys in the movie actually used the toilet in the house where I grew up. My son is physically well beyond the potty stage, but for some reason—could be genetic, could be testosterone—he remains firmly entrenched in its vocabulary.

I finally got to bed at midnight and dreamed I was at a Starbucks on *Gilligan's Island*. I had a tall café mocha and my feet up on a little chair made out of bamboo and wicker. I was staring out at the ocean, wondering if carrots could really improve vision, when I suddenly realized my daughter was calling me.

I sprang out of bed and dashed down the hallway; Sarah and I intersected just outside her door. She was holding a big wad of her nightie up in a ball.

"What is it, sweetheart?" I asked, now fully awake.

"I'm bleeding," she peeped.

"What? What happened?"

"I woke up and went potty and. . . " she sniffed once, and her voice crumbled, "and I think my period is starting."

Her period?

"Oh, wow," I said, placing my hand gingerly on her shoulder. "Wow, Sarah."

For a second we both stood there on the carpet, shivering in the shadow of the nightlight. Katherine and I had talked briefly a time or two about the possibility of Sarah being an early bloomer. But we never thought it would happen this soon. And never with Katherine out of town.

"Where's Mommy?" she asked, near tears.

"Honey, you know Mommy's in Colorado."

Why, I thought, *why couldn't this have been an earthquake? Then we could just stand in the doorway and wait for it to go away.*

"Come on," I said, leading her into the bathroom.

I won't go into details, except to say I grew up without any sisters and the only experience I'd had with periods was what I had remembered from reading the book *Go Ask Alice.* I'll never forget that poor girl wandering down the street, dropping bloody paper towels in the gutter.

Sarah hates absolutely everything that can be secreted from the human body—perhaps this is age appropriate, I don't know. I left her with a softball-sized wad of tissue and instructions to get comfortable. Then I dashed into the master bathroom to look for help. I found a blue box with pink writing on it, and I instinctively knew I didn't want to look inside because it would be filled with paper-wrapped, sticklike objects that have always seemed mysteriously foreign. As I rummaged through the arrangement of queer-smelling bottles and boxes under my wife's sink, I remember thinking about Kotex. Do they still make Kotex? What the heck is a Kotex? A million little thoughts ran through my mind as I knocked over bottles of lotion and slammed drawers, looking for a magical answer. I put on some pants and a T-shirt and dashed back down the hallway, a half-empty box of tampons rattling in my hand.

"Here," I said, thrusting the box toward my daughter.

Her big, blue eyes were rimmed with red, and her little pink lips turned down. She was breathing heavily. I knew this wasn't going to kill her, but she's always been overly dramatic when she's sick or injured or can't have dessert. That might be genetic, too . . . from my side of the family.

"Here," I said again. "Here's some tampons."

She looked blankly at me and shook her head a little, and I realized that's the exact same face I made at the French teacher in high school.

"Take one," I said, like it was a cigarette.

"I don't know what to do with those," she said.

I remembered hearing once, years ago, in junior high, probably about the same time I read *Go Ask Alice*, that girls could only use tampons if they weren't virgins. I snatched the box back.

"Right," I said. "Okay. That's okay. We'll use something else."

"What?"

"I think we'll have to go to the store," I replied.

"But it's a school night," she whined, sounding like she might cry, sounding like she'd really bought into all those stories about needing plenty of sleep on school nights.

"I know, but what else . . . ?"

"Call Mommy."

"But—"

"I need *Mommy*."

"It's the middle of the night," I protested, gently. And then, realizing her mother was in a tent on the side of some rocky mountain, I added, "She's out hiking with Aunt Julie, remember?"

Sarah started bawling.

TWENTY MINUTES LATER, the three of us were riding in our family van, headed for the nearest twenty-four-hour drugstore in search of Kotex. There were two other cars in the Savon parking lot, a beat-up Mustang and a black Jaguar. We strolled slowly toward the bright front entrance, with Sarah walking stiff-legged, like she was on stilts. As we passed through the doors and into the store, I quickly scanned the check-out area, hoping to spot a nice, elderly woman, a grandma, a gentle, retired school nurse and mother of ten who could guide us through the bewildering aisle under the sign marked FEMININE HYGIENE.

Instead, we met the eyes of Thad, a scarred and bone-thin man in his late thirties who reminded me of a guy I once met in college, a guy who kept a world-class collection of hunting knives and dirty magazines under the sofa in his apartment. Thad had a pencil-thin mustache, and I could see the reflection of the fluorescent lights in his hair. The three of us made a beeline for the back of the store.

"Can I have one of these?" my son asked, fingering a Godzilla bubble-bath bottle.

"No," I said. "Come on, we want to get out of here."

We passed rows and rows of pastel boxes covered with pictures of legs, hair, backs.

"I can see that lady's bottom," my son chirped.

"Kotex . . . Kotex . . . Kotex . . . " I scanned aloud, under my breath.

"Kotex! Kotex! Kotex!" my son shouted, at the top of his lungs.

"Eric!" Sarah whined.

"Eric!" I growled.

A large man in a blue jacket glided past the end of the aisle. I wondered what he was doing here in the middle of the night.

"What's he doing here?" my son asked, loudly.

"*Shhh!*"

Finally, we found some boxes that looked like they might have what we needed. Sarah insisted I hurry up while I read the back of the box to be sure.

Suddenly, my five-year-old snatched the box from my hand and took off running. Sarah and I both bolted for him, but I got there first and dug my hands into his shoulder, a little too hard. He yelped.

"Let's go," I said firmly, heading toward the front of the store.

Sarah and I walked on, but Eric held his ground.

"Eric," I whispered, loudly, from the end of the aisle, "Let's go.

Come on, let's go. Now. Right now." He crossed his arms and shook his head, and I started counting. He came when I hit two and three-quarters.

I set our selection down on the counter at the check-out area. Thad didn't touch it. He picked up a ray gun and shot a beam of red light at the box, and then he looked at me and then at my daughter. I felt my skin tighten. I also noticed, behind the counter, a small sign advertising a discount on prophylactics. I wondered what my wife was doing at this same moment.

By the time we got home, Eric had fallen asleep, so I carried him up to bed. Sarah headed for the bathroom. A few minutes later, I met her there.

"How's it going, sweetheart?"

"Fine," she said, softly.

"Those things work okay?"

"Yeah," she said, "I think so. My tummy hurts."

I pulled her close to me and gave her a long hug and a kiss on the top of her head.

"You want a Tylenol?"

She did, and she took one. Then I walked her into her bedroom and turned on a little flower lamp she keeps in one corner. It's a dim light. I sat down on the bed and pulled the covers up around her and tucked them under her chin. I brushed the hair away from her forehead and walked my fingers down along the covers, atop her arm.

"Congratulations," I whispered.

She smiled meekly, then silently mouthed the words "Thank you" and "Daddy."

I sat there for five or ten minutes, watching her fall asleep, looking around her room at her drawings and books and knickknacks. I felt the emptiness in the house, the silence and stillness of the night air. I also felt like crying, something I hadn't done in a long, long time.

Homework Assignment

Connie E. Curry

I HAVE ALWAYS considered myself a highly qualified homework assistant. I am a pro, as a matter of fact. As my son steadily progressed toward middle school, I refreshed my memory on fractions, proper grammar, how gravity works, and where Finland is on the map.

So, when my thirteen-year-old son unpacks his homework assignment for the day, I am sure I can gather my skills and help him. He sits down at the kitchen table, and I peer over his shoulder as I am peeling potatoes. He is to define twenty words.

"Piece of cake! Ryan, this is not a difficult assignment," I say, relieved that it is not a science project. I still want him to believe that I am smarter than he is. After all, he is a mere child of thirteen; I am a grown woman, with an education and life experience. I know it was Isaac Newton who discovered gravity. Wasn't it something to do with an apple falling from a tree?

"But Mom, I don't understand these words. I can't even pronounce them," he whines.

"You just want to go outside to play. We have to do your homework first."

As I look over his vocabulary words, my mouth drops. Oh, no. When it comes to being the homework helper, I have finally met my match. Orgasm, masturbation, ovulation, hormones, uterus, conception, sexual intercourse . . . and then I see it: *wet dream*. And they call this health class!

I start to panic. Where is his dad? Isn't this a guy thing? And why is "wet dream" one of his words to define? Isn't that slang? I bet I won't find it in my *Webster's Dictionary*.

Besides, why does this sweet, innocent child need to learn these words now? He likes baseball, cartoons, and Pop-Tarts and thinks girls are stupid.

After much consideration, I decide to have confidence that the teaching staff knows what is best for my child, and yes, of course, it is time for him to learn some facts about life.

As discreetly as I can, without being too technical, I help him define each word and try to answer directly when he asks questions.

When we arrive at "wet dream," I skim through his worksheet.

He says, "Oh, heck, Mom, I know this one! I do that all the time!"

I look out the window to see if his father is coming yet. I sigh, my heart races, and I keep in mind what Dr. Ruth says: "Masturbation is normal and healthy."

Therefore, in a calm voice, I simply reply, "Oh, you do? Well, I guess you don't need my help finding the definition."

I turn to finish dinner and try not to cry. I want Ryan to be in diapers and crawling again. I want his father home, now. I want to weep.

He closes his book and darts outside to play. His soccer ball has been calling his name. I quickly look down at his definition. It reads: "Wet dream: When you slobber on your pillowcase during the night while sleeping."

Who says Dr. Ruth knows more than I do?

Letter to a Daughter at Thirteen

Barbara Kingsolver

HERE'S A SECRET you should know about mothers: We spy. Yes, on our kids. It starts at birth. In those first months we spend twenty-three hours a day trying to get you to sleep, grateful you aren't yet verbal because at some point we run out of lyrics to the lullabies and start singing "Hush little baby, don't be contrary, / Mama's gonna have a coro-nary." And then you finally doze off, and what do you think we do? Go read a book? No, we stand over your cradle and stare, thinking, God, those little fingernails. Those eyelashes. Where did this perfect creature come from?

As you grow older, we attain higher orders of sneakiness. You're playing dolls with your friend, and we just pause outside the door of your room, *hmm-mm*, pretending to fiddle with the thermostat but really listening to you say, "Oh, my dear, here is your tea," as you hand her a recycled plastic Valvoline cap of pretend tea, and our hearts crack, we are such fools for love. We love you like an alcoholic loves gin—it makes our teeth hurt, it's the first thing we think about before we open our eyes in the morning—and like that, we take little swigs when nobody's looking.

These days I watch you while you're sitting at the table concentrating on algebra, running your hand through the blond curtain of your hair. Or after I've dropped you off at school and you've caught up to your friends, laughing, talking with your hands while your shoulders and hips rest totally at ease in the clothes and style you've made your own. I stare, wondering, How did I wind up with this totally cool person for a daughter?

You have confidence and wisdom beyond anything I found at your age. I thought of myself, at thirteen, as a collection of all the wrong things: too tall and shy to be interesting to boys. Too bookish. I had close friends, but I believed if I were a better person I would have more. At exactly your age I wrote in my diary, "Starting tomorrow I'm really going to try to be a better person. I have to change. I hope somebody notices." My diaries, whose first pages threatened dire punishment for anyone who snooped into them, would actually have slain any trespasser with pure boredom: I resolved with stupefying regularity to be good enough, better loved, happier. I looked high and low for the causes of my failure. I wrote poems and songs, then tore them up after unfavorable comparison with the work of Robert Frost or Paul Simon. My journal entries were full of a weirdly cheerful brand of self-loathing. "Dumb me" was how I christened any failure, regardless of its source. In a few years the perkiness would wane as I began to exhibit a genuine depression, beginning each day with desperate complaints about how hard it was to wake up, how I longed for nothing but sleep. I despaired of my ability to be liked by others or to accomplish anything significant, and I was stunned whenever anyone took any special interest in me.

Turning page after page in those old cardboard-bound diaries now, reading the faint penciled entries (I lacked even the confidence to use a pen), I dimly grasp in my memory the bleakness of that time. I feel such sadness now for that girl. This superachiever who started high school by winning a state essay contest and finished as valedictorian— why on earth did she fill her diary with the word *stupid*? What could any adult have said that would have helped? When I look at my year-book photos, I'm surprised to see that I was pretty, for I certainly had no sense of it then. I put on the agreeable show I thought was required of a good girl, but I felt less valuable than everyone around me. I took small setbacks very hard. Every time I took a test, I predicted in my diary that I'd flunked it. I was like the anorexic girls who stare at their bony selves in a mirror and chant "I'm fat," except the ugliness was my very self. I chanted "Worthless me" while facing daily evidence to the contrary. I've always considered this to be the standard currency of adolescence. So it takes me by surprise when we're discussing some hassle and I sigh and say, "Adolescence is a pain," and you grin and reply, "Actually, it's not that bad."

As your maturity dawns over our relationship, I think hour by hour about how I was mothered and how I do the job myself. It doesn't explain the differences between my thirteen-year-old self and yours; I take no credit for your triumphs, nor was it my mother's fault that I was depressed. She did her best with a daughter who was surely frustrating. I remember her arguing with me, insisting almost angrily that I was pretty and talented and refused to see it. She must have rained steady compliments over my scholastic and artistic efforts. But compliments help only if one believes them. At some point before age thirteen, many girls stop believing in all praise, even when it comes straight from a mirror. For you it's different. I watch you talking with your friends, or combing your little sister's hair, or standing at the back of your orchestra and elegantly bowing the strong bass line that holds everything else in place, and I see a quiet pride that's just part of your complexion. When you were little I used to declare you beautiful, and you'd smile and say, "I know." Now you're too savvy for that. But in the kitchen after school when you've reported something tough you dealt with well, and I say to you, "You have such good judgment about stuff like that," you'll look off to the side, and it'll be written all over your face: "I know." It's your prize possession. I'd do anything to see you keep it.

When I was pregnant with you, I read every book I could find on how to handle all things from diaper rash to warning lectures on sexually transmitted diseases. I became so appalled by the size of the task that I put my hands on my belly and thought, Oh Lord, can we just back up? But the minute you were born I looked at your hungry, squinched little face and *got* it: We do this thing one minute at a time. We'll never have to handle diaper rash and the sex lecture in the same day. My most important work will change from year to year, and I'll have time to figure it out. At first I was just Milk Central, then tiptoe walking coach and tea-party referee. Eventually I began to see that the common denominator, especially as mother of a girl child, was to protect and value every part of your personality and will, even when it differed from mine.

In this department I don't think girls of my generation got such a good shake from the guardians of our adolescence. The guidebook for parents then was organized around a whole different thesis; spanking was mandatory, and the word *self-esteem* had not been invented. The supervisors of my youth loved my accomplishments until I started campaigning against things they believed in. They thought I was beautiful, but they bluntly disparaged the getup required for *my* idea of beautiful. I wasn't even allowed to say I disliked a particular food. I made almost no significant decisions about my own life: I ate what I was fed, washed dishes but never planned meals, participated in school-sanctioned activities but virtually never hung out unsupervised with my friends. The parents of my time and place worried about pregnancy, drinking, and car accidents—as well they should have, since these shadows would fall sooner or later across the lives of most of my peers. I participated in a mind-boggling number of school-sanctioned activities but lacked time to be *me*, away from adults, just with peers. That must have looked too dangerous. As a child I'd spent endless hours poking around in the woods or playing disorganized games with other kids in the fields around our house, but once I grew breasts, my unchaperoned days were over. I felt increasingly scrutinized and failed to develop a natural ease or confidence with my peers. I was convinced that my parents would never let me grow up, so I railed against them internally but then felt guilty after, fearing they would mind-read my rebellious thoughts.

At age fifteen I was allowed to go on a trip with the high school English classes to see a performance of *Measure for Measure* in a nearby city. It was my first experience of Shakespeare (my first real play at all), and I felt elated afterward by this exposure to mature ideas and drama. But discussing it with my parents that night at dinner, I grew tense. There had been some implied sexuality in the play; my brother and I had made a pact not to mention it, but I feared somehow they knew anyway, and I was too nervous to eat. I felt sick inside, as if by watching this wonderful work, and loving it so much I'd betrayed my parents' trust in me and my own goodness.

When I went off to college at eighteen, I promptly went straight off the deep end of the social/recreational pool. It frightens me to look back on that reckless period of my life, but I also understand it perfectly. I'd been well under control up to that point, but I had no practice in *self*-control. I was extremely lucky not to damage myself in the process of learning moderation.

As penance for this close shave, I vowed early on to give you more choices than I had, so you could learn self-control in a safer laboratory than I did. The dance of letting go the reins is never easy—two steps forward, one step back. I've spent so much of my life stitching together the answers to the hard questions that it's natural for me to want to hand them down like a glove, one that will fit neatly onto an outstretched little clone hand. I try sometimes. But that glove won't fit. The world has changed, and even if it hasn't (drinking, drugs, and pregnancy are still at the top of the immediate-worry agenda), the answers will work for you only when you've stitched them together yourself.

People say it's because parents *love* their kids so much that they want to tell them how to live. But I'm afraid that's only half love, and the other half selfishness. Kids who turn out like their parents kind of validate their world. That was my first real lesson as a mother—realizing that you could be different from me, and it wouldn't make me less of a person. When you were three, in spite of all the toy socket-wrenches and trucks I'd provided in my program of teaching you that women can be as capable and handy as men, you basically wanted to be the Princess Fairy Bride. You'd have given every one of your baby teeth for a Barbie doll. I tried to explain how this doll was an awful role model, she didn't look the way healthy women should, she was obsessed with clothes, blah blah. Translation: My worldview doesn't have room for Barbie in it, and I'd be embarrassed to have her as a houseguest. I wouldn't give in on Barbie.

Then, one day you and your friend Kate were playing in your room, and I was spying just outside the door (yep, fiddling with the thermostat again) when I heard you say, "My mom won't let me have Barbies. But you know what? When I grow up I'm going to have *all the Barbie dolls I want!*"

Yikes, I thought to myself. Soon afterward, Barbie joined our family.

That was a stunner for me. Believe it or not, it was the first time I really pictured you as a someday-grown-up, completely in charge of yourself (and your menagerie of dolls). Eventually I'd have zero power over you, I realized, so this might be a good time to start preparing for it by shifting from 100 percent to 99 percent control.

Let the Barbies come, and let you handle the Social Impact. You did, and along the way you probably learned a thing or two about physics: What happens when you shoot Barbie from a paper-towel tube? Also about disabilities: When the puppy found your abandoned Barbie party and left it looking like the Plane-Crash Barbie Close-Out Sale, I made you keep most of the Barbies, asking, "If your friend lost a leg or a hand, would you throw her away?" (The headless ones we laid to rest.) And I learned to say, when you dressed yourself in bridal veil, roller skates, rouge, and a tutu, "Wow, you have a really creative sense of style." I've never lied to you. I didn't say I thought you looked *good*, just creative. Maybe that's why you believe in my compliments now.

Every mom has to set limits, but that's never been so difficult with you. When you want something that I truly think will do you harm, I explain my reasons, and then usually let you have a *little* of it (except if it's illegal, or skydiving) or give you permission to abide by your friends' mothers' rules when you're at their houses (case in point: watching TV). Though you may not notice it, I'm keeping an eye out to see how long it takes you to decide you've had enough. Except for that one time when you put your whole face in the birthday cake, your judgment has proven exceptional.

All your life you've been apprenticing for adulthood. I recognized that when you were in preschool, learning how to be social: having feuds with girlfriends, then forgiving or sometimes moving on. One week they'd shun you, the next week you were queen bee while somebody else suffered. It tore me to pieces to watch, but I knew I couldn't save you. You were saving yourself, slowly. In fifth grade, it suddenly got harder: A boy started picking on you, mostly trying to embarrass you with sexual innuendo. Oh, man, did I want to walk into that classroom and knock some heads together. But I took a deep breath, knowing that even this—*especially* this—you had to learn to do for yourself. I was scared. It was my hardest mom event so far, and I didn't want to screw it up.

And it is *so* easy to screw this one up. When I was a teenager, the story I got from the world around me on how to behave with boys was a real song and dance, which boiled down to this: Boys want only one thing, which is to have sex with you, which is too nasty even to talk about, and it's your job to prevent it. They're also stronger than you and likely can do what they want, but if they succeed in raping you it's your fault, actually, because it was your job to avoid getting yourself into a position where you couldn't stop it. Also males are more important, they run the world, and if you want any kind of happiness or power, you're going to have to win their favor. Got it? Ready, set, go.

The day I sat down with you on your bed to talk about the Grade 5 boy problem, I felt as if I were jumping out of a speeding car, blindfolded, into a snake pit. I took a breath and said, "This is a good time for you to start learning how to handle inappropriate male attention." I told you three things: First, if you ever got truly scared, I would intervene. Second, it was fine to get really pissed off at this boy, because everybody deserved the right to go about her business without being harassed; the creepy feeling you had was *not* your fault, it was his. Third, boys are just people like us, and if they behave sensibly they can be very cool to be around—even in a physical way if that is your inclination, when you eventually feel the confidence and fondness to be with a guy like that.

Finally, I told you that unfortunately there would always be some guys who feel it's their gift to behave as irritants and scoundrels. You'd run into this many times in your life, and a classroom was a safer place to learn to defend yourself than, say, a college bar or a workplace.

Then we practiced role-playing. I wanted you to say, "No, I hate that, you make me sick, go away." You found it hard; your tendency was to be polite, even coy. I realized, with agony, that the world had already begun teaching you that girls should be pleased with, or at least politely tolerant of, male attention of any type. I tried not to hyperventilate. We practiced some more, you learned to take a very firm tone, and you made it through fifth grade. *I* learned what you were up against. It was not too early for me to begin thinking of you, and talking with you, as a transitional woman, with important disputed ground to claim for yourself on the map of equality. You've kept me posted on the main events in the boy-girl arena, and so far I've been impressed with how you've handled them.

I didn't do nearly so well myself, as a teenager. My first kiss happened the summer after I turned fourteen, at band camp—a school-sanctioned activity during which I was theoretically chaperoned every minute of the day. I met a cute boy named Dave who showed a flattering interest in me, and one evening when we were meant to be washing dishes he asked me to go outside instead, and mess around behind the so-called mess hall. I was scared to death; I went. Our kissing was nowhere near as graceful as the movies, with an icky dampness factor that seemed categorically not too different from washing dishes, but I felt thrilled to have been chosen. After camp ended I never heard from him again because, of course, we'd had no friendship, and I felt creepy about my tryst. I'm lucky he didn't expect me to go beyond kissing. I hope I'd have resisted (I'm pretty sure terror would have helped me out), but I'm sad to admit I can't say for certain. It took me years to get over being flattered and flattened by any kind of male approval. My first relationships in high school and early college were stunted by my inability to separate my interests from my boyfriend's. The guys who did time in that capacity during those years were invariably sweet; it wasn't as if they *meant* to ignore or malign me. It was just that I felt such pressure to remain coupled that I swallowed my own will to keep from rocking the boat. *Like* what he *likes, do* what he *wants*: I couldn't imagine just acting like myself in the company of a guy.

I see a lot of girls your age who are just the way I was then. I remember hearing one of your friends declare helplessly, "I can't say no to boys"—in the sixth grade! I feared for her future reproductive life. But not yours. I can see very well that if a male friend didn't take an interest in the things you care about, or wasn't respectful, you would use your remarkable charm and wit to lose him, fast. Or at least tell him that, as I heard you recently say, "he's not *all that* and a bag of potato chips." It's a huge relief to me. I look forward to meeting the guys you'll date.

You already know a lot of the things I had to teach myself in my late teens and early twenties. What saved me was nothing short of a complete transformation, the kind of soul-shattering revelation that some people find in religious salvation. *I* found it in the novels of Doris Lessing, Maxine Hong Kingston, Margaret Drabble, and Marilyn French, along with the words of Betty Friedan, Germaine Greer, Gloria Steinem, Robin Morgan, and lots of others. I began to find these books my last year of high school and then really sank into them in college, reading the way a drowning person breathes air when she finally breaks the surface. I stayed up late reading; I sat all day in the library on Saturdays reading. Every word made sense to me, every claim brought me closer to being a friend to myself. These writers put names to the kinds of pain I'd been feeling for so long, the ways I felt useless in a culture in which women could be stewardesses but the pilots were all men. They helped me understand why I'd been so driven by the opinions of men. I was not stupid; in pandering to male favor I'd been pursuing what would be the smartest possible route to power in, say, Jane Austen's day, when women couldn't own property or vote. But these writers allowed me to imagine other possibilities. There are still many countries where women have to go the Jane Austen route: Muslim extremists stone women to death if they show their faces and declare their opinions in public, but here you'll only get some hate mail for it. The worst that was likely to happen to me, if I began standing up for myself at age nineteen, was that some guys who handled me with less deep concern than their auto transmissions would probably cut bait and run. This loss could be endured; that was all I needed to know. When my despair finally crystallized as anger, my conversion was rapid and absolute: I cut off my long hair, I began to dress for function rather than sexiness, I got mad at whosoever tried to bully me by virtue of unearned privilege—and I discovered there were guys who actually *liked* me this way. I joined a women's group on campus, then found a church that was more forgiving of personal lapses of judgment than of larger, social ones, such as war and hunger. I began working with migrant farm workers in central Indiana whose problems were larger than mine: They had no clean water or shelter. I learned more about the Vietnam War than I'd previously gleaned from *Reader's Digest.* By concentrating on what I could do to make things better for people who were worse off than me, I taught myself to feel significant. Word by word, day by day, I revised the word *stupid* out of my journal.

The premises of feminism—that women are entitled to do any kind of work men do, for the same pay, and to be accorded an equal measure of social respect—must seem obvious to you. But in 1973 these items were just barely on the agenda. The first time I suggested to my father that a woman could be president, he got a pained expression on his face just thinking about a woman having to go through that mess. He asked me, as delicately as he could, to consider what a disaster it would be if we had a war, and the president was on her menses. Both of us were acutely embarrassed, and that was the end of that. (It didn't occur to me until years later that most presidents are elected well past the age when menses would be an issue.) When I told my parents about an older college friend I admired who intended to keep her name after she got married, my mother offered sadly, "Any woman who'd do that doesn't love her husband."

My parents, in telling me of these and a thousand other limitations on my gender, weren't trying to hold me in contempt. They were merely advising me of the ways of the world—which, in 1973, held me in contempt. Since then they've changed their minds about many things, including my keeping my last name, which is now also yours. (And if you ever run for president, I'm positive Dad will vote for you.) But the persistence of misogyny in the world outside our family is not forgivable, and it makes me crazy. Why is it, for instance, that on the popular teen radio station, all the women are singing about guys who treat them like dirt (or, on a more optimistic note, declaring the jerk must go), while the men are chanting, sometimes literally, "Die, bitch, die"? It scares me that boys listen to this stuff; it scares me more that *girls* do. I can't tell you what to listen to, I know. To this day I get a buzz when I hear the first notes of "Lay Down Sally," probably from all the warnings I received against its morals and grammar. But if you're going to listen to these guys, *listen.* Eric Clapton was singing to me, "You are *so* the best, I can't stand for you to leave the room." I'd just once like to hear that from some rapper. One of the best gifts you ever gave me was when you turned off Eminem and started listening more to Sheryl Crow and Alanis Morissette on your CD player. I think—I hope—you did it not for me but for you. Because you didn't need "Die, bitch" as bedtime music.

I know that some girls of your acquaintance worship Eminem. Some are already doing drugs and having sex with guys because they need male approval that badly. I understand that perfectly, because of how *I* was in my teens. I wish I could tell them it's not too late yet: If they can just yank it back for a minute and find some little island of pride, there's hope. But it takes believing in some larger space for women in the world than they can presently see. For me, that belief came from the right books, because I happened to revere the printed word. Even more, it was finding and joining a huge, heady current that allowed me to believe I could change things a little—that I could fight back against what made me angry, in some way that was real and grown-up. Piercing and branding one's flesh or getting pregnant or getting AIDS is *not* fighting back, even though it may feel like it from the inside. From the outsider's point of view, these things make a display of self-loathing, which is the opposite of fighting back—it's a score for the opposition. I know, because I used to hate myself, and now I don't.

You never did, it seems. You like who you are, you work hard at whatever you do, you're kind to your friends, you show compassion for the world. You're a person I'd choose as a friend even if we weren't related. I actually like the ways you're turning out different from me; your confidence and smart-aleck wit inspire me. I was impressed, the day we were listening to the presidential campaign and the one guy started pandering to the audience, when you rolled your eyes and said, "What a suckup!"

If I'd said that about a presidential candidate when I was your age, I would have gotten it for disrespecting authority. So I had to ask myself, *Am I allowed to laugh at what she just said?* Answer: Yes. I agreed with you totally; he was groveling for the vote. I can't insist to you that all authority is worthy of your respect, because much of it is not. In five years you'll have to see through all the sucking-up and vote for your own president. Why *shouldn't* you start practicing now?

Every authority has its limits. I find myself defusing the menace of maleness by viewing it as a source of fascination. I study it constantly, not trying to learn how to *be* that, just trying to understand it. To say they run the world just doesn't cover it, because we do, too, in our less material way. Not in terms of real power, of course; it's impossible to imagine a reverse Saudi Arabia, in which we walked around doing whatever we pleased while forcing our entire male population to vacate themselves from public life and wear black cloth sacks with sideways slits for their eyes. We could never get them to do it; they're devoted to being in charge of things, and we seem unable to whip up any zeal for treating people like that. It's hard even to imagine a tradition of fine art in which naked men would recline on picnic blankets while fully clothed women looked on. Recently an artist in Colorado tried to communicate (especially to men, presumably) how it feels to have our sex so constantly and casually appropriated: She created a display of colorful penises pinned to a clothesline. The surfeit of masculine heebie-jeebies wrought by this little demonstration made national news, and lasted only days before a man broke in and destroyed the installation. I hope the artist has sense of humor enough to see that she made her point perfectly. Men rule, but in general seem to lack our fortitude.

And yet in some way or other their whole lives long, heterosexual guys are knocking themselves senseless to get our attention, and you can't help being charmed by the parade of nonsense. One of the most absurd, sexiest, most entrancing things I've ever seen took place right outside my study window. I was trying to think of a metaphor or something, staring out there into the mesquite woods, when suddenly my eyes snapped to focus on some movement: two rattlesnakes rising up together, face to face, as if they were being noodled up out of two snake charmers' baskets. Moving slowly with muscular, sinuous strength, they levitated nearly the entire front halves of their bodies, twisted themselves together, tussled a little, and finally slammed to the ground. It resembled arm wrestling. I ran to get everyone else in the house, and we all watched this thing go on for nearly an hour, the two snakes rearing up again and again, silently entwining and then throwing themselves to the ground. We called our friend Cecil, the Arizona reptile expert, who informed us that arm wrestling wasn't such a bad analogy: These were two male snakes doing a dance of combat to win the favor of a female that was surely watching from somewhere nearby. We scanned the brush carefully from behind my window—these snakes were not even thirty feet away—and there she was, sure enough, stretched out languidly under a bush.

Then all at once, after innumerable tussles, according to some scoring system invisible to human eyes but unmistakable to the contestants, one guy won. The other slunk quickly away, and Sheba came sliding out into the open, with no eyelashes to bat but with love clearly on her mind, for off she slithered with her he-snake into the sunset. The greatest show on Earth.

WHEN YOU, MY DEAR, were about two and a half, I carefully and honestly answered all the questions you'd started asking about reproductive organs. For several months thereafter, every time we met someone new, the unsuspecting adult would tousle your adorable blond head, and you'd look up earnestly and ask, "Do you have a penis or a vagina?"

If you are *ever* tempted to think my presence is an embarrassment to you, please recall that I stood by you during the "penis or vagina" months, July to September 1989. I wasn't sure I'd live through them or have any social life left afterward. I gave you a crash course in what we call "polite company" and harbored some doubts about whether honesty had really been the best policy.

What I see now, though, is that honesty *was*. Manners arrive in time; most girls are gifted enough at social savvy to learn the degree of polite evasion that will protect their safety and other people's dignity. But before anything else, you've got to be able to get the facts. Penis or vagina? I couldn't possibly tell you it wasn't to be discussed, or didn't matter. It matters, boy howdy, does it ever. Barbie or Ken, Adam or Eve, pilot or stewardess, knuckle sandwich or mea culpa, scissors, paper, rock, War and Peace. It's a very reasonable starting point. So begins the longest, scariest, sexiest, funniest, smartest, most extraordinary conversation we know. Cross your fingers, ready, set. Go.

The Thong Question

Nina Gaby

"THE BOYS IN OUR school only like girls who wear thongs," says my daughter one day in the car. It is a random statement, out of nowhere. But she now has my attention.

We are transplants to Vermont, where the commutes are longer, the stars are brighter, and the kids are more precocious.

I murmur something indistinguishable from the undercurrent of the public radio station that underscores most of our long drives these days. My daughter is thirteen, which means she doesn't talk to me as much as she used to. I am grateful for this piece of information despite the fact that it is going to drown out an interview on *Fresh Air* that I have been waiting for.

Buying myself a little more time, I fiddle with the volume button, reluctantly turning it down. How do I address her statement? When did our conversations begin to include the word "thong"? I am a woman who has spent fifty years trying to avoid anything that even resembles a thong. When she was little, we called them "wedgies" and they were a bad thing. I have also spent the last decade of my life as a psychotherapist and have gone down the verbal rabbit hole with many folks far more skilled than my daughter. At least, I hope they were, because I am clueless as to what she wants or needs from me right now.

"Wow." I opt to remain neutral.

She answers with a noncommittal "Yeah."

The ball is in my court now. I say "Yu-uck" in the trendy, disyllabic way that I hope brings some credibility to my half of this conversation. I have tipped my hand with the "yuck," but I have not fully committed to an attitude.

I can still go several ways here. One wrong move and I lose her.

I think about switching the radio volume back up so I can enjoy the rest of the ride home, but my therapy training haunts me. I know what this desire to immerse myself in the comforting sounds of NPR is called—avoidance. I keep my hands on the steering wheel, and the volume stays low. Rationalization won't work here, either.

A check in the rearview mirror reveals my daughter staring intently out the window, gently biting on her lower lip. The look on her face tells me I have to address her unwelcome announcement from school. But, dammit, I don't want to.

Thongs are so much more than underpants. Thongs are the line drawn, as it were, between child and woman. Between cool and not cool. Between safety and expectation. A metaphor for the tightrope my kid traverses as she tries to look disinterested, staring out the window, seeing her life fly by as she ponders the whole thong question. These are the defining moments of early adolescence.

I remember my own seventh-grade year as if it were two days ago. For me, a nerdy twelve-year-old, it was about whether to ditch the red-and-white-striped glasses and the corduroy jumpers that my grandmother bought for me and my mother found so flattering. It was about taking that step into black stockings and tight black skirts and finding a big plastic purse (also black) with room for economy-sized hairspray, Cover Girl eyeliner, teasing combs, slam books, and all the other accoutrements of survival as a teenager in 1963. The whole world was changing, and I was paying very close attention. For me, it was agonizing but necessary to abandon my family and emerge black-garbed, nicotine-stained, white-lipsticked, beehived, and very separate. I missed them, and it was painful. But it was necessary.

My parents anesthetized themselves nightly with my father's special brand of very dry martinis. ("Just pass the bottle of vermouth over the glass," I can still hear him say, "just a whisper.") I recall them reviving only on report card nights or for selected family functions, when they would notice how completely dark, sexy, and inappropriate I had become. I learned their avoidance tactics only too well, and from that point on, it was only a quick slide into my own mad chemical rush as I paid personal homage to the decade of experimentation. And to a couple subsequent decades.

Karma notwithstanding, I now take sober pride in my determination to Deal With Things. It is a distinguishing characteristic that is being severely challenged by my sudden life as the mother of a thirteen-year-old girl. I wish to God I could shrink myself into the car radio and chat with Terry Gross, maybe even ask her a few questions, and listen to her calm, comforting replies.

The back seat remains quiet. My daughter is still waiting for a response. Here are my options: If I ask my daughter if she wants a thong, she will immediately feel inadequate and say she's too fat. Or the blatant sexuality of the idea will send her off into a diatribe on how she hates boys, and what am I talking about? Or, if she doesn't have a boyfriend, then will she hate me more because she thinks I am worrying about why she doesn't have a boyfriend?

If I take the responsibility and tell her that she can't get a thong, assuming she even wants one, it will alleviate some of the anxiety for her, but then she will think I am a fifty-four-year-old dinosaur who is not as cool as the other kids' mothers. And my worst fears will then be realized: She will rebel and start purging her dinner or snorting heroin or behaving in any of the other myriad ways I have observed in the children of uninformed and overly controlling parents during my years as a professional standing waist-deep in the misery of other families.

If I ask how the seventh-grade boys even know that the seventh-grade girls are wearing thongs, she will burst forth with disdain. "Mom. They wear their pants low enough that the thong band goes above the waistband. God. Don't you know anything?"

So I opt for the safety net of the classic therapist's tactic. (I know it is a cop-out, but I didn't sit in the discomfort of both sides of the therapy chair for twenty-plus years to not allow myself to cop out in an emergency. I have earned this.)

"So, uh, how do you feel about the whole thong thing, honey?"

Silence. Did I offend her? I turn toward the back seat, ready for anything.

And this is what I see: The warm Vermont light streaming in to illuminate her perfect skin as she sleeps with the utter peace of a napping three-year-old. Her face is pressed to the window as if against a car seat, lashes long and luxurious on her sweet, round cheeks. Her mouth is softly open in a plump oval, lips a classic strawberry red, as if longing for a thumb to suck.

I want to stop the car, just to hold her. For one more moment, let her still be mine. Instead, I turn off the radio and slip in her favorite Evanescence CD so she can wake up to its cacophonic lullaby.

Baby, It's A Wild World

How to Lie to Your Parents

David Carkeet

GIRL, YOU'RE GOOD at this, and they're not. That's point number one. You're good at it because you lie all the time, not just to them but to everybody, even your best friends. You exaggerate, you distort, you flat-out lie. If you didn't, you'd be dead. But your mom and dad hardly ever lie, so they're not only bad at it, but when they see a mouth moving, they assume the truth is coming out of it. Ha!

Don't sit down. They'll say, "Sit down. We need to talk." Don't do it. Stay on your feet. If they say, "I asked you to *sit down*," lean your butt on the edge of a table or on the arm of the sofa. If they get all mad at that, you'll have to sit, but you've already worn them out. (They tire easily.) You're ahead of the game, and you haven't said a word yet.

There are two kinds of "sit down" talks, the you-did-something-bad talk and the we're-not-going-to-let-you-have-fun talk. The first is about the past, and my advice here might surprise you: Let it go. Let them do their thing. Confess, apologize, and take your punishment. You see, your best argumentative tool—I mean besides bluster and volume and body heaves and percussion from contact with walls and furniture—is vagueness, and the past lacks reliable vagueness because it's full of actual facts. If you lie about these facts and are found out, you put all future lies at risk. Dad in particular is nuts for facts—haven't you seen him reading those twenty-pound history books? The facts'll kill you. Accept them, admit to them, and take a short-term hit for the sake of the long-term gain of future fun.

That brings me to the second kind of talk. Basically, your life consists of huge pleasure on the other side of a fifty-foot wall named Mom and Dad. Any fun you have in mind immediately fires up their question engine. Don't accept that they have the right to pump you. Of course you've *got* to accept it—what are you going to do, move out?—but you need to make them feel that they're stomping all over your rights as a human being when they ask you even one question.

Let's say they've given you their boring summons ("We need to talk") because they've filled up their no-lives with some snooping about your plans. It's time for you to select your weapons. The "everyone" argument is an old one, sure, but the reason it's been around so long is that it works, especially if you know how to meet challenges to it. When you tell them that everyone is going to this party or whatever it is, Mom will instantly say, "Everyone?" Then she'll give a name. This is her favorite thing in the world to do. She'll pick someone real upright as a test case. When she names her, stare blankly for a long time, then squint your eyes and say, "*Who?*"

Say it like she just named some pharaoh who's been dead for centuries. She'll fumble then, wondering if she got the name right. Then do this: Make a face like you finally figured out who she means and softly say, "Oh my God," signaling that this particular girl could not be more irrelevant to your life. What, was she in a Brownie troop or something with you a decade ago? (That's pretty good, actually. Go ahead and use it.) Mom will suddenly feel out of touch with your life, and she'll fall silent while she regroups.

Dad, meanwhile, will be working the details—who's driving you, where, what kind of car, miles per gallon, weather conditions, ETD, ETA. He's a pilot, basically, and no one's going to smoke in *his* toilet. Dad's good at spotting contradictions, too. "You said Stephanie's mother was driving you home, but you also said Stephanie had to leave the party early—how do you explain that?" Don't give him that kind of opening, especially when you're working a completely false story. Let's say you told them that you're going to help Jen babysit a kid in her neighborhood and then sleep over at her house when you're actually doing something rather different: going with some older boys to an unsupervised party at Jen's parents' cabin in the country. Here comes Dad, all frowning: "You're babysitting with Jen? But when you stopped babysitting last summer, you told us all of your friends had stopped too, and you gave Jen as an example." Obviously your mistake here was giving them that earlier information. It's best not to tell them anything at all about your life. But you already know that.

When you create your cover story, remember the old saying— "A liar must have a good memory." The way they're losing it, it's clear who's got the upper hand here. Every time Mom wanders into a room and says, "Now, why did I come in here?" you should go *Yes!* because she's slipped another notch.

And remember that these talks are about the future, where confusion reigns supreme. Build your mighty castle on the clouds of confusion. Be specific, but present all details as mere options, pending developments out of your control. Your parents can't make that fatal phone call to check on your story if they can't figure out who to call. So tell them maybe Abby's mom is driving you, but maybe not—after all, you think Abby's little sister has a make-up soccer game that night, but it might be rescheduled because of a school fair or something . . . Tell them you'll let them know when you find out for sure what's going on, and it doesn't hurt if you share their anger about the uncertainty—people can be so frustrating, blah blah blah. In fact, be mad through the whole talk, and of course the best way to pull this off is to be mad all the time, at least when you're home.

Language tip: "Trust" is a great word, as in "You don't trust me." Of course, they'll have examples from the recent past that they use as "grounds" for not trusting you. But the standard comebacks will do here. "That wasn't my fault," for example, or "Oh my God, I can't believe you're still talking about that." Either of these will get them thinking. This is why they're so weak. They respect you. They take your words seriously. You couldn't ask for a bigger soft spot in an enemy than that.

If you find yourself stuck for an answer, use their sentences as raw material for sentences of your own:

Them: "Last time you told us you'd be at Megan's, and you ended up at Nina's."

You: "And this time I'm telling you I'll be at Jen's, and I'll end up at Jen's."

Them: "We have the right to know what your plans are."

You: "And I have the right to *my own life!*"

The beauty of this approach is twofold: (a) the repetition of a pattern saves you invention time and allows your mouth to motor at a speed that will make them want to end the talk and take a nap, and (b) each of these pairs is a closed set, and your echoing of their sentence ends the discussion of that particular point. Eventually, they'll run out of points.

Don't be afraid to use distraction just because it feels so pathetically obvious. It works, believe me. In the middle of everything, point to the cat and say, "How come she's missing some fur on her belly?" Mom will drop to the floor and spread the cat out like a wrestler going for the pin. Or frown and put your hand to your stomach, like you've got a pain there. Dad'll think, "Period?" and have a bunch of complicated thoughts that'll shut him down for a while.

And here's a good trick for the advanced. Carry your cell phone in a back pocket, and be prepared to work it secretly. If things blow up in your face, press the speed-dial number for your home phone. The ringing in the house will break the rhythm. If Dad says, "Let the machine get it," say you are expecting a call. Seem real unhappy about that—it's the call of a lifetime, and he's standing in the way of it. You'll all sit there and wait until the machine gets it. If your cheery voice gives the greeting on the machine, all the better, especially if you recorded it when you were younger and innocent. Mom and Dad will hear the voice and remember how good you were—and maybe still are! When the greeting ends, secretly push the hang-up button on your cell phone and give Dad a hard look: The caller didn't leave a message, so the call of a lifetime is in ruins.

Now, let's say you win this round—and you should after everything I've told you—and you go to this party. Let's say it's a disaster. There are people there you've never seen, people you've never even imagined existed, people who blocked the doors and refused to let anyone leave, and you and Jen hid in a back room and you called home and your dad came and—God—actually *rescued* you. Now, does this mean you're in a worse position for your next negotiation?

Girl, if you think that, then you're just unteachable. Here's the obvious way to handle it, though I shouldn't even have to tell you. When the next illegal event rolls around—and I hope it happens for you real soon—simply say, "Do you guys seriously think I didn't learn my lesson last time?" Give a shudder, and they'll give one too, and before you know it you'll be perfectly positioned for a night of fun, fun, fun.

The Dark Side of the Moon

Rebecca Boucher

ANNIE, MY LEAN and lovely sixteen-year-old, floated down to the breakfast table early one Saturday morning. I realized as I checked the clock—it was eight thirty in the morning—that there must be a cross-country track meet that day or she never would have been out of bed at such an hour. She calmly spread cream cheese on a toasted bagel and told me she would be taking the subway, by herself, to her meet. It was taking place in a huge park at 242nd Street in the Bronx, a significant subway ride from our Brooklyn home.

"I've been there plenty of times," she said, wiping her hands on her jeans. She took a bite and chewed for a minute. "I'm fine alone."

She was wearing a T-shirt, size ten-year-old-girl, that my sister gave her (this by way of explanation that I would never have bought the thing myself and yet felt compelled to let her keep it). It was vivid green and had a map of Kentucky on it. It read, GETTIN' LUCKY IN KENTUCKY.

I didn't quite know how to explain to her that a girl who looks like her—which is to say like a rose about to burst into full and glorious bloom, a girl who makes you want to reach out and touch her skin to see if she's real, a girl who is about five minutes away from being a woman, a girl who turns heads on the street and makes her father's stomach churn—simply does not ride the subway by herself from Brooklyn to the Bronx while wearing a teeny tiny T-shirt that reads GETTIN' LUCKY IN KENTUCKY. At least not my girl. She well might know the way, but knowing which train to take is not the only trick to this journey. I need to make whatever small attempts I can to keep her close and safe.

I WAS REMINDED, while she sat there chewing, of a not altogether different incident involving her thirteen-year-old brother. He had emailed me from school that week. His message managed to strike a tone halfway between enigmatic and breezy. It read, *will and me are going to hear white stripes at roseland on tuesday night i'll do my h-work 1st promise.*

I had responded: *Do you think I'm Helen Keller? Nothing in your run-on sentence worked for me: not "Will and me," not "White Stripes," not "Roseland," and least of all "Tuesday night." You're not going. It's not only because you use terrible grammar, but that is a contributing factor.*

I should have added, *You're not going because I am not ready to have you, too, fly away.*

I do feel deaf and blind and like I can't quite communicate. My children and I are no longer occupying the same worlds. Sometime when I wasn't looking, they each left the fenced-in pasture I carefully built for them and are now wandering around unfettered in a world I have never visited. While I don't see this world, there is evidence of it in every corner: the fact that they would contemplate going to Roseland on a school night, for example, or taking the subway from one end of New York City to the other.

Another indicator is that I don't really and truly know where they go anymore, not in the way I am used to. Previously, their friends had all been children I watched grow up. I had held their hands on field trips, shared potluck dinners with their parents, sat around with their mothers with coffee cups in our hands, waiting for the magician to finish the balloon animals at their birthday parties. I knew the layout of each of their houses, I knew their siblings' names, I knew their mothers' decorating styles. That was elementary school.

Now, in high school, new kids have appeared on the scene: kids with no faces, addresses I can't picture, last names I still have to look up in the school directory. As teenagers, my kids surely don't need me to stay for the birthday party or playdate. I definitely don't have to coax them to go to a new child's house. My children disappear into the homes and lives of these people, and I have no hook, no way to reel them back in.

They use words I don't understand. They have an incredibly annoying habit of answering questions with the non sequitur "I win." They laugh at things I don't really think of as funny, like how I gesture with my hands when I'm angry or how my enunciation suffers when I am emphatic. They won't ski with me anymore. When I ask them why, they say, "Because." I can hear their voices as they talk to each other from their separate rooms, holding conversations across the hallway, but when they hear my footfall on the stairs, they go quiet. On long car rides, they listen to their iPods, earphones huge around their ears. I can't penetrate their world even when we are within two feet of each other.

MY FRIEND MARCIA, a mother of three teenagers, has an apt analogy. "Look," she says to me one day, "they are on the dark side of the moon now. We have to figure that we set them up, before all this happened, with enough good sense to make the trip. They are somewhere where we can't really see them anymore. We can only hope they make it around to the other side."

That's what I don't like: We can't see them anymore. It makes me want to catch hold of their forearms and make them stand still. I want to look into their eyes and ask them what it's like out there in space. I know, though, that they won't tell me. It's not out of contrariness or obstinacy; it's because they truly can't tell me. Not in a way that I can understand. In the meantime, while they make their orbit, I will continue to make my small, and increasingly meaningless, efforts to keep them safe. I will drive Annie to her meet and put my foot down as long as I can with her brother. I can't stop them from growing up any more than I can stop the moon from orbiting.

And even as they disappear, being pulled by powerful tides into this dark territory, I know I can't follow them.

I Definitely Inhaled

Daniel Glick

IN 1970, WHEN I was fourteen, my mom and I had a "theoretical" discussion about marijuana. Sitting at the kitchen table, we exchanged stories about what "people said" it was like to be high. She volunteered that she had heard some people got "cotton mouth," when an area from the lips to the larynx felt like it had been drained of all fluids. I countered that I understood some people got "the munchies," an uncontrollable urge to empty refrigerators and pantries of all nutritional content.

After the conversation, I recall wondering why she knew so much about it. She probably wondered the same about me.

Soon after our chat, my dad's parents arrived for a visit, and my mom's tension level elevated in direct proportion to the approaching hour. (She didn't get along with my grandmother.) Just before my grandparents arrived, I made a fateful decision. I walked into my mom's bedroom and offered her a package wrapped in a ribbon, which she looked at quizzically.

"It's my last joint, Mom," I said. "But you need it more than I do right now."

She hesitated, then laughed. "Well, we might as well smoke it together," she replied, and we went into her bathroom to light up.

She took a hit, then passed it back to me. I did the same. Then I passed it back to her.

My grandparents' visit went swimmingly.

THREE DECADES LATER, I had a family of my own, with a young daughter and a son cusping on puberty. After some wandering years, I had become a journalist, first as a national reporter with *Newsweek,* and then as a freelance writer in Colorado. One day, my son, Kolya, came home after a seventh-grade drug-education class and either had been misinformed or had misconstrued some of the information. Somewhere in our conversation, he mentioned that pot was a hallucinogen, and I took it as a signal that it was time to "talk to your kids about drugs," as the ubiquitous full-page newspaper ads suggested. We sat on his bed, his room festooned with posters representing a four-subject catalog of current interests: teen sex goddesses in low-cut outfits and suggestive poses, snowboarders in sick midair poses, skateboarders in sick midair poses, and punk bands in simply sick poses.

I matter-of-factly walked him through the mind-bending array of drugs—where they came from, what they did to your brain, how addictive they were, everything I could think of: marijuana, hash, hash oil, acid, mushrooms, mescaline, peyote, speed, ecstasy, airplane glue, angel dust, downers, cocaine, speed, cough syrup, heroin. As a baby boomer who came of age in Berkeley of the early 1970s, I was an authority on many of these, either from personal experience or my friends' experiences.

After that initial trial balloon of smoking pot with my mom, my parents and I rarely got high together. But I had continued a sporadic relationship with certain mind-altering substances into adulthood. For years at a time, even a decade at one point, I had nothing more than a social drink. Then I would acquire a small stash of marijuana and tap it occasionally as I would a bottle of expensive single-malt Scotch. Like many in my demographic bulge now finding themselves raising teenage kids, I knew I would eventually face a day of reckoning when I would have to confront how much to reveal about my own past—and current—experiences and experimentation.

I had definitely inhaled.

During our drug talk, Kolya decided my day of reckoning was nigh. He listened fairly attentively as I walked him through my purposefully clinical listing of the pharmacological and physiological properties of various mind-expanding contraband.

Glad we had this talk, son.

"Dad?"

"Yes."

"Have you ever taken acid?"

Pause.

How do I answer that question?

"Yes, but only a couple times. I didn't like it." The simple, unadorned truth.

Next Kolya question: "Have you ever smoked pot?"

"Yes."

And that was that. He, apparently, hadn't yet learned the journalist's prerogative of the follow-up question.

A couple days later, I checked in while I was driving him to soccer practice. "Kolya, how was it for you to hear that I've taken acid and smoked pot?" I asked.

His answer confirmed that I had done, if not the right thing, then at least something vaguely correct. Kolya shot me a sideways glance and deadpanned: "I'm just glad you didn't lie to me 'cuz I wouldn't have believed that an old hippie like you never smoked dope."

I scrambled to educate myself about the teen drug thing. Evidently, the people running the antidrug public awareness campaigns knew they would be talking to people like me:

For many parents, a child's "Did you ever use drugs?" question is a tough one to answer. Unless the answer is no, most parents stutter and stammer through an answer and leave their kids feeling like they haven't learned anything—or even worse, that their parents are hypocrites. Yes, it's difficult to know what to say. You want your kids to follow your rules, and you don't want them to hold your history up as an example to follow—or as a tool to use against you. But the conversation doesn't have to be awkward, and you can use it to your advantage by turning it into a teachable moment.

—From the Partnership for a Drug-free America

Most of the information stressed the mantra "Just Say No." But I knew that in my own experience, there was a difference between occasional drug use and drug abuse. I just didn't know where the line could be drawn with my own kids. I knew that pot was much stronger today than it was when I was a teen, and I personally knew far too many kids who had gotten into deep trouble—and even died—from drugs. How could I make a judgment about what route Kolya might take? Was there middle ground between "Just Say No" and "Go Right Ahead"?

I asked Kolya if he had ever tried smoking dope, and he said nah, he hadn't. How about his friends? There was a rumor that some kid in eighth grade had done it, but basically, none of his friends did, either.

That summer between seventh and eighth grades, I took Kolya on a backpacking trip with my twenty-year-old nephew and an old friend of mine. Evidently, as we scrambled over granite passes in Yosemite, my nephew had told Kolya that a lot of people, including grownups that Kolya knew, still smoked pot. Probably even Uncle Danny.

Thank you, nephew.

A few weeks after the backpacking trip, I was tucking Kolya in when he posed a new and inevitable question: "Do you *still* smoke pot?"

This one was tougher to answer. I had read about kids who were told by school officials to turn in their parents for drug use, and although I didn't think Kolya would do that, I wondered what he would do with the information.

I swallowed, opted for the truth again. "Sometimes."

I also sensed that Kolya had gone a lot further in the six months since our last conversation, and it turned out that he had. He said he still hadn't tried smoking anything, and I believed him. But more of his friends had tried marijuana, and he was getting really interested. He was barely thirteen. I really didn't want him starting now.

We talked more about drugs. I told him that I suspected that he was going to be under a lot of pressure, or at least he'd soon have the opportunity, to try it himself. I also told him that I thought he was much too young and that it was a bad idea. I knew that the "Just Say No" message would seem particularly hollow now that he knew about my early experiences, combined with what I knew about his temperament.

So I tried a different tack: "Just Say Not Yet."

I told him that the pot these days was extraordinarily strong, that it messed with your memory, that his brain was still developing, and while I didn't expect that he'd wait until he graduated from college to experiment, I wanted him to hold off for at least a couple more years.

As I PICKED MY WAY through this particular parenting-an-adolescent minefield, I had little help from Kolya's mother. I was divorced and a single dad to both Kolya and his nine-year-old sister, Zoe. On a family camping trip a few years earlier, my wife of fifteen years announced that she had fallen in love with somebody else, wanted a divorce, and would be moving out of state to live with her new girlfriend. I abruptly found myself raising our two young children in the messiness of our marital aftermath, alone.

With their formerly full-time mother a thousand miles away, I felt confounded by the complexities of raising a girl who would begin wearing a bra in fourth grade and overwhelmed by the challenge of shepherding a punk-rocking boy through adolescence. I found myself dragging Kolya out of groggy sleep for middle school in the dark, making his breakfast, filling out field trip forms, double-checking to see if the orthodontist's appointment was today or tomorrow. I'd coax him out the door just in time to wake Zoe for the winter morning ritual of hot cereal, asking her exactly what she wanted in her lunch, reminding her to ask her friend what she wanted for her birthday gift for this Saturday's party. I'd wonder what to make for dinner, would there be just enough milk for tomorrow's breakfast, did I really have to attend the soccer club's annual meeting, how come I just washed the dishes last night and it already looked like the kitchen had been assaulted by a Class V hurricane.

At times I worked myself into a homicidal rage, blaming every indignity of my current life on my ex-wife's departure, every Kolya and Zoe meltdown on the psychological trauma of being maternally abandoned. I didn't see how I could learn to become a respectable single dad, earn a living, and simultaneously keep the household running. I knew the teen years were right around the corner, as surely as Zoe knew that googly monsters lurked under her bed.

A YEAR TO THE DAY after the divorce was final, my older brother Bob died of breast cancer. After these dual shocks set in and Kolya turned thirteen, I decided that I needed to do something drastic: I conceived an epic, half-year, around-the-world trip with my two kids. I decided that perhaps we could take solace in each other while visiting some of the world's great natural wonders: the Great

Barrier Reef in Australia, orangutans in Borneo, the Himalayas in Nepal. I decided that I wanted to forge a new family of three, using adventure as our crucible. I knew I needed to do it quick, before the chance was gone forever.

"Before they're gone" became my mantra for this trip—with a triple entendre. The first, literal meaning directed me to show Kolya and Zoe this planet's amazing animals and environments before overpopulation, poverty, global climate change, pollution, and development maimed or destroyed them. The global devastation of wild places during my lifetime mirrored my other losses, touching me no less profoundly. Kolya and Zoe, raised on flashes of music videos and DSL Internet downloads, had only the barest suburban inklings of the natural world that I clung to as my spiritual core. Perhaps I could help them make a deeper connection during this trip.

The trip's second goal instructed me to seize this otherwise inglorious personal transition to spend time with my children before they left my reconfigured single father's nest. In the fall, Kolya would start eighth grade and Zoe fourth, and I could already tell they would become fledglings too soon. I wanted to get to know them; I wanted them to know me. Learning about who they were and how they saw the world seemed to me to be the best hedge against the oncoming rollercoaster of adolescence.

Lastly, the big "before they're gone" loomed especially large: After witnessing my brother's untimely death at forty-eight, I knew viscerally that I possessed no guarantees regarding how long any of us would be around. Electing to do something extraordinary, I asked the kids what they thought about circumnavigating the globe.

To my surprise, they were enthusiastic. Even the increasingly diffi-
dent Kolya signed on—as long as he could bring his skateboard.

On July 6, 2001, we found ourselves winging our way to
Australia, where we would begin our odyssey. I observed the kids
snoozing in their seats as we passed the equator, my gaze resting on
Kolya, who, now fully engaged in puberty, seemed to grow as he
slept. We wore the same shoe size already (11½), and by the end of
the trip he would complain that mine were too small for him. He
was opinionated about any subject he opined upon and dismissive
of any subject that didn't interest him. His blue eyes already drew
adoring glances from teenage girls, but he didn't yet realize he was
going to be a looker. He wore his dirty-blond hair short, buzzed
tight on the sides, invariably covered by a backward baseball cap.

Kolya in particular was in a very dicey spot, I felt, slouching into
his teen years reeling from the divorce and Uncle Bob dying. Like
most teenagers, he wanted nothing more than to be grown-up
completely. But like most thirteen-year-olds, he still wasn't ready to
fend for himself. Sex, drugs, and rock 'n' roll were fast becoming the
currency of his consciousness. And I desperately wanted to slow
him down. Or so I thought.

Upon arriving in Australia, we rented a camper van and cruised
along the far northeastern coast, in Queensland. Several weeks into
the trip, I arranged to meet a family friend for the weekend—
whose name, for reasons that will become obvious, has been
altered. Darren Peabody was a wealthy fifty-something professional
who evidently lived his life on his own terms. He greeted us like

long-lost relatives in his elegant home on the Gold Coast, not far from Brisbane. I had, in fact, only met him once before and had no idea what was in store for us.

As soon as we walked into his home, furnished in contemporary wealthy bachelor, the kids were smitten. After living so low to the ground with their tightwad dad, the barrel-chested, gregarious Darren was a divine manifestation. For lunch, he barbecued up some of the best steak any of us had ever eaten and uncorked a bottle of French burgundy that I would have reserved for my fiftieth wedding anniversary, had I stayed married long enough to have one. He poured wine for the kids without asking me if I minded, and we feasted on his veranda while he talked nonstop of his plans for us.

He had a neighbor, a single mom with three kids, and we would all go jet skiing that very afternoon. Later we would all go out for dinner, the next day we would have a sunset picnic, and if we were available to return the following weekend, he would take us out on his houseboat.

The single mom, we'll call her Samantha, arrived with her three kids, a fourteen-year-old girl, a twelve-year-old boy, and another girl Zoe's age. The eldest, Francesca, was at a glance far more sophisticated than Kolya, with a European dad and an Aussie mom. She had traveled between the two continents enough to be thoroughly world-weary before she could drive. She began offering opinions about what Darren was wearing, the music we had on the stereo, and the distasteful school her mom made her attend. All the while checking Kolya out from the corner of her eye.

And vice versa.

After dinner the kids scattered. Darren went into his bedroom and returned with a pipe and something that was obviously not tobacco. I was, to be honest, aghast. There was no reason to believe the kids wouldn't burst into the living room at any moment. I was not at all ready to have the drug talk with Zoe yet, nor to explain the upcoming compromising situation to Kolya. I told Darren that I was uncomfortable getting high in front of the kids. He told me I didn't have to smoke if I didn't want to.

I tried again, telling him that I'd been trying to give Kolya the message "Just Say Not Yet," and that I didn't want to mix him up by flagrantly adding, "But I'm going to right now." He blithely said that he thought Kolya seemed mature enough to handle it. He lit up and passed it to Samantha, who offered it to me. I abstained.

The kids never came in, and when I could talk about this to Kolya later, I learned that he didn't have a clue what the grownups were doing.

He was busy with other business.

The next day, we set off on our promised picnic excursion. Darren, Samantha, and I sat on a bluff talking while the kids played on the beach. A half hour later, Francesca's sister and Zoe came back with an excited announcement: Kolya and Francesca were "sucking face."

To my astonishment, Kolya and Francesca appeared holding hands, and stopped within eyeshot to suck some more face. Kolya looked very pleased with himself, and Francesca clung to his hand as if she had found a handful of gold coins in the sand.

Kolya had told me of a stray kiss during a truth or dare game, and I think there had been a spin the bottle smooch or two, but I was pretty sure this was his first bona fide affair. I tried to act like it was no big deal, even as Francesca's sister and Zoe buzzed as if they had seen their first R-rated movie.

The next day, we bid everybody farewell. Kolya and Francesca sheepishly held hands, and I discreetly got in the car so they could say their goodbyes. We told Darren we'd be back the following weekend for the houseboat cruise.

WE SPENT THE WEEK surfing in a town a few hours from Brisbane, with Zoe and I teasing Kolya mercilessly about his *liaison dangereuse* with Francesca. We returned the following weekend to meet Darren at the marina. We provisioned up and pulled out in his cabin cruiser. It was a beautiful, warm afternoon with light winds as we headed for the South Stradbroke Islands.

Just before dusk, we anchored in a channel between two small islands. Darren cracked open a bottle of wine; we ate and admired the sunset. As we watched the stars come out, the kids recounted our travel stories to Darren with appreciable excitement, which he shared.

Darren went below and rummaged around for another bottle of wine and emerged with what appeared to be his pipe, again. I quickly took Zoe below for bed. As I passed Darren in the galley, I made a fateful decision. "Go on. If he wants to, let Kolya try it."

I read a bedtime story to Zoe and half smiled, half cringed as I heard Kolya coughing from the deck. Zoe was so tired she drifted off to sleep as I was reading.

I shut Zoe's book quietly and headed up to the deck, unsure what would happen next. I looked at Kolya, pointed to the pipe on the table, and whispered, as Darren was peeing off the back of the boat: "Did you???"

Kolya shook his head in an emphatic "No." Then he shook his head the other direction, grinning wildly, with an even more emphatic "Yes." I know that he was caught between not wanting to lie and not wanting me to get angry because he'd violated my "Just Say Not Yet" policy. Darren apparently hadn't told Kolya that I had given the green light.

"It's okay, Kolya. I told him it was okay this time."

He grinned again.

"Do you feel anything?" Still whispering.

Emphatic "No" again.

"Wait a little."

And then Darren came back, loaded the pipe, and handed it to me.

I looked at Kolya. Another moment of truth. Then I took a hit. Somehow, it seemed right, with the waves lapping, the offshore breeze brushing our faces, and the moment offering itself like a spontaneous gift.

OVER THE COURSE of the trip, Kolya and I found opportunities to just hang out and talk. I watched as he became more curious about the world in measured doses, and he soon began what would become a regular refrain during the rest of the trip.

"So, Dad," he would begin, his warm-up to questions that ranged from Uncle Bob's high school football career to how the Vietnam War started. I loved these discussions as we walked through improbable places together—from jungles in Borneo to the streets of Paris.

Some days he would ask about the history of civilizations, about how *Homo sapiens* evolved and developed tools and agriculture. Other times he would ask about the divorce, about my youthful indiscretions, about what Grandma and Grandpa were like as parents. I told him the story about smoking a joint with Grandma. He could barely imagine it.

After 9/11, which happened when we were in Singapore, he extended his questions to include the bombings, the Muslim world, Osama bin Laden, and American foreign policy.

As we left Singapore en route to Vietnam, I watched Kolya and Zoe board the plane. After several months of foreign travel, they were now well-seasoned globe-trotters, with dirty daypacks and battered earphones. They handed over their boarding passes as if they were getting on a school bus rather than boarding a plane to Ho Chi Minh City. The four of us inched down the gangway in a crowd, and I realized we were the only Caucasians on the flight. The kids didn't seem to notice, and Kolya helped an elderly Vietnamese woman whose rolling suitcase caught on a protruding piece of metal.

I could see them deepening their understanding of and connection to the world around them, even as the world became less comprehensible all the time. In turn, I was deepening my understanding of them, watching as they found their way with increasing confidence.

AFTER OUR RETURN to Colorado, Kolya quickly finished middle school and headed for high school. I had immediately let him know that our trip rules did not translate to home rules. During his freshman and sophomore years, however, it became clear that Kolya did not take my "Just Say Not Yet" message to heart. I found some solace in the fact that he talked with me about his experimentation, even though I worried that he was smoking more dope than I thought was healthy.

Still, he managed to get good grades, play on his school's soccer team, and participate in the household chores. We had some notable blowups, several incidents that ended in him being grounded, repeated you-can't-tell-me-what-to-do/oh-yes-I-can-because I'm-paying-the-bills discussions, yet still managed to keep the lines of communication open.

He turned sixteen, grew taller than me, beat me at one-on-one in basketball, got his driver's license, and applied for a semester abroad program for half of his junior year that would take him back to . . . Australia.

ALMOST EXACTLY THREE years after our departure for the world tour and a month before he would leave for Australia, Kolya, Zoe, and I planned a whitewater rafting trip in Colorado's high country. We spent the evening before our river excursion at a mountain cabin. Zoe went straight to bed.

I had brought up two beers to wind down from the drive and invited Kolya to have one of them with me on the deck.

"Do you want to have a hit, too?" he asked me. Like my mom did with me so many years ago, I hesitated, then said yes.

We sat under the stars, perched on a log, and passed the pipe. We talked about his upcoming trip, about what a passage it was for him to be heading off on his own. We chatted about the impact of our round-the-world trip, about our lives, about Uncle Bob. Then we didn't talk at all and watched shooting stars and lightning illuminating a distant ridge. I put my arm around his broad shoulder and kissed his cheek.

"I love you, you know that?"

"I love you, too."

"I'm sure going to miss you," I said, tears suddenly streaming to my eyes.

"I'll be back," he said.

I hugged him again, rested my arm on his shoulder, and we turned our heads in unison to follow a streaking star heading toward the horizon.

Their Bodies, Ourselves

Helen Klein Ross

SEE MY TATTOO? A friend extends her forearm to me. She has just come back from a vacation in the islands with a black blot on her arm in the shape of a lizard. It's only henna, she says, but I'm getting one done just like it for real.

She means to amuse me, or perhaps means for me to share her delight in her free-spiritedness at the age of sixty, but I feel socked in the stomach. My daughter just got a tattoo, I say by way of explaining my lack of enthusiasm.

Which place did she go to? my friend wants to know, and I feel the force of a one-two punch.

MY DAUGHTER GOT a tattoo the month she turned fifteen, on a day she told me she was meeting friends for pizza. She did meet friends for pizza, but after that she and a friend took a cab to the Village. This friend looks even younger than my daughter does, and now every maternal instinct rises in vain to prevent those two impetuous, unblemished girls from walking up and down Eighth Street, peering into the windows of tattoo parlors, scouting for one that looks seedy enough to overlook the fact that they are, indisputably, minors.

When I think of the man who beckoned them into a shop, who took my daughter's fifty crumpled dollars, who watched my daughter lower her jeans, who bent my daughter over a chair, who told her to squeeze her friend's hand for the pain, who breathed on that soft, downy place at the small of her back as he stabbed her again and again with a needle, who repeated each step of this with her friend (and with how many other misguided children?), I feel myself capable of seizing his neck and squeezing the breath out of him.

I DID NOT DISCOVER the tattoo right away. When she and her friend finally walked through the door, having been out of cell phone reach for some time (this had given me a couple of frantic hours), they said they'd been detained by delays in the subway, a lie I believed readily, not only because delays were so common in those first few months after 9/11 but because my intuition was short-circuited by the waves of relief I'd felt upon seeing them turn up alive. Her friend lives in the suburbs and was staying the night. I trembled with gladness that I did not have to phone her father and break the news to him that his daughter was missing (as, moments before, I had imagined myself doing).

They were hungry and requested a child's dinner—chicken and mashed potatoes—a request I was deliriously glad to oblige. They watched a couple of videos (I was surprised and relieved that they did not want to go out) and went to bed early. When I went in to wake them the next morning for pancakes, they were asleep on their stomachs, each clutching a stuffed animal. For the pain, I now realize.

Several weeks later, while I was chiding my daughter for some minor infraction, she turned her back and bent to get something from a bottom drawer. The waistband of her jeans pulled away from her skin, and I saw for the first time, in the hollow this made, a blue-black scroll on her lower back. It looked like—a doodle.

It's only henna, she claimed. But when that did not spare her my closer inspection, she confessed that it was, indeed, a tattoo; she'd gotten it that day on the way home from school. The inked skin was calm and porcelain white; I knew (from the movies) that freshly tattooed skin was inflamed. She told me the truth only after our exchange grew so heated and rancorous that it culminated in actual physical struggle. I found myself pulling her hair, as if to yank the truth out of her. I was roiling with anger and hurt and betrayal in a force I had not felt since I was a teenager, at war with my mother.

She was grounded for weeks, a consequence she accepted with surprising equanimity.

In our discussions during those weeks we spent at home with each other, she said that she was sorry for lying, she was sorry for getting her friend into trouble, she was sorry for going to a hole in the wall, but she was not sorry—not sorry at all—for getting a tattoo.

SHE THINKS IT IS beautiful. (It is a leaf.) She does not want to remove it. Her father thinks we should remove it, whether or not she is willing, and make her foot the bill for the process. I wish away the tattoo as strongly as he does but cannot agree to remove it without her consent, an act that would be as repugnant to me as are other ways to appropriate a young woman's body.

It's your body, I said to her grudgingly, wishing I didn't have to entrust something so precious to the care of such an irresponsible party. And so she agreed to accompany me to a laser surgeon for a consultation regarding tattoo removal. This laser surgeon had been recommended to me as the best in New York, perhaps in the world. Certainly, his fees attested to this. The cost of consultation—showing him her tattoo and hearing whether or not it was removable, and if it was removable, how easy or complicated the process would be—was $275.

We spent a long time in the waiting room, filling out forms. There were at least ten pages to read and initial, each covered with words in archaic English that attempted to expunge the doctor of responsibility in case of a mishap.

The room was filled with anxious-looking men and women of all ages, none of whom had tattoos that were visible. A badly blonded woman in her early thirties popped in and out of her chair continuously to cross the room and consult with the receptionist because she couldn't make sense of the forms. (I couldn't make sense of them, either, but saw no reason to try. Being married to a lawyer has taught me that boilerplate forms exist to deter frivolous lawsuits; in case of wrongdoing, they are not actually binding.)

A slight, ponytailed man seated next to the woman accompanied her on her next trip to the receptionist. I saw that they'd sat a young child between them, who was now left alone, small and uncertain, on the sofa. His mother yelled at the child from across the room, Don't you go now and start your blubbering.

I raised an eyebrow at my daughter: *Behold your destiny.*

We were shown to an examination room, where we waited for the doctor to make his appearance. The doctor looked preposterously young, young enough to still be in college. Sensing my incredulity, a reaction he must frequently encounter, he hastened to mention that he was *not* the famous doctor, but the famous doctor's assisting physician. He was there to explain tattoo removal, which was presumably too tedious for the famous doctor to do.

I was anxious to hear what he'd have to say. My daughter sat fully clothed on the examining table, contemplating the floor. But I could tell that she was listening, too.

The process would entail four to eight sessions, each lasting five minutes. A laser gun would trace the tattoo. After each session, the skin would scab, and when the scab came off, the tattoo would be faded. It was impossible for him to be certain of how many sessions would be required before the tattoo disappeared entirely, but such an outcome, in her case, was almost certainly possible. She is lucky, he said. Her skin is fair. Her tattoo is black. Red is the hardest color to remove. He told us that they can't usually get red tattoos out. He said this with a sorrowful shake of his head, as if he were confessing to personal failure. He guessed her tattoo would take five or six sessions, each costing the price of the consultation.

At this point, the famous doctor came in. He shook my hand vigorously and confirmed everything that his assistant had said.

Any questions? he asked.

I thought.

Is it painful?

Nothing compared to how it feels going on. They didn't give you anesthesia, did they? He turned to my daughter, who shook her head. That's how they get away with tattooing kids, he said. The legal-age laws are for anesthesia.

I couldn't think of another question.

The famous doctor gave my hand a final pump and then redirected us to the waiting room, where we stood in line for a while to pay.

THREE YEARS HAVE passed, and I've stopped hoping that she'll decide to remove it. She is convinced that she'll keep her tattoo forever, that it is emblematic of the person she is, like the walls of her room, which are covered with words to poems and songs, and photos of young men in the poses of sun gods, whose near-nakedness seems ironic to me, as they labor in the service of pur-veyors of clothing.

What's the big deal? I hear my free-spirited friend ask—my friend who, years ago, turned her henna lizard into a bona fide tattoo. And part of me concedes that she's right.

Making a permanent mark on one's body seems as endemic to my daughter's generation as oversized overalls and unisex hairstyles once were to my own. Any doubt I may have had about this was dispelled by our recent college tour. It seemed that every student on campus bore some sort of indelible mark. Even the Ivy League tour guides (presumably kids considered the most presentable) bore, along with their charm and good cheer, evidence of self-mutilation—if not a tattoo, then a stud in the nose or a glint in the navel or a constellation gleaming from the upper rim of an ear.

Yet, as unremarkable as my daughter's tattoo may be to others, I still can't catch a glimpse of it without flinching, can't stop trying to recall the night twelve or so years ago—there must have been a last time I gave my daughter a bath. I would have been hurrying, my mind already on phone calls to make or paperwork to finish as I hastened a blind, wet cloth across the small of her back, heedless of its shining, temporal perfection.

Baby books explain that an infant assumes her mother's body to be her own, that it takes several months for a baby to learn where her own body stops and her mother's begins. The books say nothing about how much longer it takes a mother to absorb this difficult lesson.

Only Rock 'n' Roll

Stevan Allred

I SURVIVED THE MOHAWK. I survived the homemade tattoo and the pierced lip. I survived Marilyn Manson and the year my son refused to go to school. I survived the nights he never came home.

He's seventeen now, and wears bondage pants with ripped-out knees over long johns with ripped-out knees over long johns with knees. His hair is buzzed off short, and it's the light-brown-to-blond color he was born with, nothing you'd notice in a crowd. He has an X tattooed between the thumb and forefinger of one hand, and it's got that jailhouse look, but it's small, just a series of blue dots his ex-girlfriend put there to match the ones she tattooed on herself. At least he didn't get it in jail.

He still lives at home. When I count the days until he turns eighteen, it's because I am afraid he will leave. I used to count them because I wanted him gone.

Arcadio was named for a character in a Gabriel García Márquez novel, but everyone calls him Cado. He's a sexually active, pot-smoking high school dropout who likes to sleep until noon.

I'm still looking for a bumper sticker that says MY KID ACED THE GED TEST. We went to a therapist together for a few sessions, and the therapist's favorite line, delivered to me with deadpan British irony, was "You must be very proud." I white-knuckled the years from eleven to sixteen. The only thing that got us through was rock 'n' roll.

Mine is not a household where many things are banned. When my son tore holes in his clothes and wrote Kurt Cobain's name on the toes of his Chuck Taylors, I let him. Hair dyed in all those Manic Panic colors was no big deal. When he announced that he was bisexual and so were all his friends, we talked about safe sex. I told him that if he wanted to rebel, he was going to have to take a hard right. Try Young Republicans, I suggested, try born-again Christian, try joining the Marines.

We're progressive folks who believe in the free exchange of ideas in an open marketplace, and that includes our family lives. Back in the '80s, when Tipper Gore pushed to have those warning labels put on CDs and records, I thought she should be forced to write the First Amendment on the blackboard a thousand times.

Of course, that was before I had children of my own.

MARILYN MANSON FIRST ENTERED our household through my son's best friend. Evan had wheedled his parents into buying him Manson's *Antichrist Superstar*, and he brought it with him on a sleepover. I had some vague notion that Manson was the leading purveyor of something called "shock rock," that he was considered extremely controversial, perhaps even dangerous, by the media, but I didn't have a clear idea why.

Rock 'n' roll has gone, during my lifetime, from fringe music to elevator music. It's been a long, strange journey for a form of expression that is as rooted in antiparental rebellion as it is in rhythm and blues. It's a journey that has forced certain practitioners of the form to find ever more outrageous ways to perturb the parents of their listeners. In the late '90s, Marilyn Manson was simply the latest and most extreme example. I knew all this, and I knew that singling Manson out as something I would not allow would only make this forbidden fruit all the more attractive.

But it wasn't really about Marilyn Manson; it was about Cado. He was starting to hang out with a large knot of punked-out kids who frequented Pioneer Square in downtown Portland. Some of them were runaways, street kids who appeared to Cado to have successfully slipped the noose of school and family obligations. There were also a few older punks whom Cado called "the Crusties," men in their thirties who lived in squats or under bridges, some of whom were junkies. It was a scary scene, and a magnet for middle-class kids like Cado, who identified punk as the one true response to our consumerist culture. We lived far enough out of town that Cado's access to the downtown scene was limited, but there was no question in my mind that I could still lose him to that scene all too easily.

Cado was also doing poorly in school at the time. He had discovered the vulnerable underbelly of my progressive hide, that very soft, very white place that said, "What I really care about is your education." He was a thirteen-year-old, self-styled anarchist who knew exactly where my buttons were, and he wouldn't stop hammering on them. Not only was he unfailingly nasty to his step-mother, not only did he steal things and tell ridiculous lies to cover it up, but he absolutely refused to do any homework. Grounding him, taking away privileges, letting my voice crack and my eyes fill with tears when I told him how disappointed I was in his behavior, none of this fazed him. Cado just didn't give a shit.

I was terrified that I was raising a sociopath.

His art project for school that year was a drawing of a burning cross with Satan horns resting on an anarchy symbol. The frame was a ply-wood cutout of flames. In that context, Marilyn Manson's *Antichrist Superstar* looked a whole lot like a five-gallon can of gasoline.

So I banned Marilyn Manson. I refused to allow my son to buy the CD with his own money, and I did this on the extremely shaky ground that he wasn't old enough. This ground isn't shaky because it's an unreasonable judgment—it's quite often perfectly reason-able—but because it feeds into the adolescent's notion that the adult world is an elaborate conspiracy designed to keep him a child for-ever. He thinks no one understands how grown-up he really is, and he's left with either subverting that judgment or going into open rebellion against it.

My son chose both.

SOMEHOW, WE GOT THROUGH the year. The thing that I clung to was our ongoing conversation about rock 'n' roll. We had been talk-ing about rock 'n' roll since he was eight years old and spent his summer vacation listening to my collection of Beatles CDs. We talked about Nirvana and Kurt Cobain's suicide. We talked about the '60s, the Doors concert I went to when I was fourteen, the Rolling Stones. We talked about punk rock. Rock 'n' roll was the one area where he accepted me as an authority.

Gradually, it became an area where I accepted him.

By eighth grade, Cado showed more effort at school, got into trouble less, began to take some interest in getting enough work done that I wasn't constantly on his case. After his first-term school conference, in which the written evaluation from his teacher began, "Is this the same kid I had last year?" I looked for a way to reward him.

He asked me to take him to Seattle to see Rancid, a hardcore punk band who had stellar street cred because they played a lot of all-ages shows, and this meant they cared more about the kids than they cared about the money. Cado now wore his hair in a devil lock, like the lead singer of the Misfits, another favorite band. He wanted a Mohawk, but I said no. When he asked me how old he had to be before he could get a Mohawk, I gave him my standard answer, the same one I used for tattoos and piercings: forty.

His devil lock was a single lock of hair that hung down the middle of his face all the way from his forehead to his mouth. He kept it there with some hair-stiffening product that he mixed with Elmer's glue. The rest of his hair was buzzed off a quarter inch long. It was a hairstyle that was bizarre but instantly recognizable to punk kids in the know. It was all I could do to walk down the street without cringing when people stared, first at him, and then at me.

The Rancid show was sold out before we ever heard about it. I told Cado not to worry, that if we wanted to get into the show bad enough, if we led with our absolute conviction that we were going to get in, if we took a rock 'n' roll attitude toward the problem of getting a ticket, everything would work out.

THREE AND A HALF HOURS before the Rancid show starts, there are fifty people in line. The hairstyle of choice is a Mohawk, the jackets are leather and covered with shiny steel studs, and the piercings are plentiful. Cado reads these kids as hardcore, the real deal. They're not posers, he tells me. "Poser" is the worst, most damning insult in his arsenal of hipper-than-thou sarcasm. But not one of these hardcore kids has an extra ticket.

We hang out, circling the block and asking everyone we see, "Got an extra ticket?" A couple of times, we just miss. We're not alone in our quest, and anybody who has a ticket to sell is quickly surrounded. Two girls who claim to have been the first ones in line when the tickets went on sale offer us their tickets for three hundred dollars apiece. We decline.

Cado and I split up. We can cover more territory that way, and he doesn't have to be seen with a forty-seven-year-old geek who's dressed like he works in a hardware store. Cado is wearing a leather jacket covered with buttons and studs and patches with the names of his favorite bands. On the back is one of his old cloth diapers, where he's written "The Subhumans" and carefully drawn their band logo. The diaper and the patches are neatly stitched on with dental floss.

Kids are approaching the club from all directions, and it's a postmodern punk revival freak show of the first order. It's hard not to read the black lipstick, the handcuffs hanging from their belts, and all the metal studs in their outfits as armor. After years of exposure, their facial piercings don't make me cringe anymore, but then I see a three-inch-long steel barbell pierced through the back of someone's neck, and it makes me shudder. I keep asking kids if anyone has an extra ticket, and I force myself to look into their eyes if they will let me.

It's easy to read their thoughts when they take me in. They blink, their eyes widen, and a question appears in face after face: "What the hell are you doing here?"

IT TAKES THREE HOURS to find two tickets. We're searched before we enter, and the security people confiscate my fountain pen on the grounds that it could be used to stab someone. Cado has to surrender the six-inch-long safety pin that is part of his outfit. The security guys are polite but serious, and they don't crack a smile when I thank them for believing that my pen really is mightier than a sword.

The club is like dozens of clubs I've been in, a dark, low-ceilinged room jammed with kids, and it's easy for Cado to lose himself in the crowd. I watch him until my view is blocked by a kid with an amazing Mohawk. This Mohawk is eight inches long, absolutely stiff, its individual strands combed out as finely as whale baleen. His hair is bleached blond from the roots out and dyed blue at the tips. The rest of his head is shaved perfectly clean, and the narrow strip of Mohawked hair has precise edges. The Mohawk stands up like the crest of a tropical bird and gives its wearer an exotic, avian beauty.

He is the cock of the walk. His appearance is shocking, bizarre even, but the magnificence of this display of personal adornment is undeniable. To my surprise, I am attracted rather than repulsed, and something inside me shifts. Cado's devil lock and his leather jacket are art. The drama and originality of his visual statement is something I could be proud of.

THE STAGE IS AT one end of the club. There's no place to sit except on the floor, and nobody is sitting on the floor. It's smoky, and when the bands are playing, the crowd is sucked in tight, sixty or seventy people deep.

I am the oldest person in the place by two decades.

AFI comes onstage dressed in all black. The lead singer, Davy Havoc, is a handsome dark-haired man-child in the charismatic vein of Elvis Presley and Jim Morrison. His band tears the place up, and the mosh pit is a frenzy of kids pushing and shoving each other. I'm not close enough to see if Cado is a part of it, but I'm pretty sure he's there. It's not the first mosh pit I've seen, but it's the most violent, and I'm glad that the security guys have been so thorough.

I keep pushing my way forward, in part because I want to locate my son, but also because I want to study the pit. The violence of it baffles me, and this frenzy of pushing and shoving is both threatening and fascinating. Mosh pits are mostly male zones, located at the intersection of anarchy, testosterone, and loud music. They look like a fight breaking out, but somehow, one never does.

The shoving is done at chest height for the most part—it's meant to move people without knocking them down. The pit has a permeable perimeter that allows people to step in and out of it. There's laughter out there, and sweat, and a kind of physical bliss. Someone catches an elbow in the face, but when he glares at the guy who hit him, the elbow thrower puts his hands palms up in apology, and everybody goes back to pushing and shoving, the incident forgotten.

I catch a glimpse of Cado being shoved halfway across the pit. He's the smallest guy out there, and they've got him pinballing back and forth, and he's grinning and lurching around and pushing back. He goes down on the floor, and immediately there are two or three hands stretched out to pull him back up.

It's hard not to be frightened by the violence of the pit, but the closer I look, the less it looks like combat. They are riding the crest of a wave, surfing the thin edge between moshing and fighting. The movements are radically different from the twirling, spinning, free-form dancing I learned in the psychedelic era, but their roughness is in service of the same goals: community, transcendence, personal expression.

The Who told my generation that The Kids Are Alright.

They still are.

BETWEEN BANDS, I stand in the back of the club, where there's actually some room to breathe. A teenage girl dressed in black who says her name is Tracy asks me what I'm doing there.

"My son is here," I say. "He's fourteen. I drove up here from Portland to take him to the show."

Tracy has a lot of eye makeup on, and she's wearing a spiked dog collar around her neck. She has the studded belt and the Doc Martens that are the entry-level fashion statement for this crowd. She checks my face carefully for a moment, blows smoke out the side of her mouth, and says, "I wish my dad had taken me to a show when I was fourteen."

I REPEAT THIS EXPERIENCE with my son several times over the next couple of years. His taste in music stays resolutely punk, and I take him to shows I would never have gone to on my own. We see MxPx, One Man Army, Virus 9, Anti-Flag, the Ataris. I get comfortable with Cado disappearing into the crowd. He's with other kids, some of whom I know and some I don't. If our paths happen to cross, I let him be the one to decide if we will acknowledge each other. It is a part of the bargain we've struck. Cado is on the young end of the crowd at these shows, but he wants to be treated like he's sixteen, and no sixteen-year-old punk would be caught dead at a show with his parents.

I watch parents drive up in their SUVs, drop their kids off, and drive away. Once in a while, I see another parent who stays, but it's rare, and it's always a mom, never a dad. I meet lots of kids while I'm hanging out, scary-looking kids with too many piercings and tattoos and that whole biker/punk/bondage fashion uniform. Most of them are polite and distant, maybe a little suspicious, but occasionally one will talk to me.

Over and over I hear this: I wish my dad had taken me to a show.

It is what Cado cannot say to me directly. It is all he can do to mumble thanks to me at the end of the evening. But through these kids, I learn not to be fooled by appearances. What is extreme and off-putting is also an invitation. They are challenging us both to love them for who they are and to see beneath the surface.

Underneath the piercings and the tattoos and the leather jackets, they are our kids.

WHEN CADO IS FIFTEEN, we get a chance to meet Marilyn Manson. He's coming through Portland on tour, and I have a writer friend who's done an article about him. My friend invites us to go to the show with him and to go backstage afterward and meet the Antichrist.

By this time, Marilyn Manson is no longer banned music in our home. Cado and I are having an ongoing conversation about Manson's lyrics, about his ceaseless attempts to shock the audience and the world at large, about his stance as an artist. I see Manson as manipulative and hypocritical. On the one hand, he slams our culture for being shallow and materialistic, and on the other hand, he feeds his own celebrity at every opportunity by making outrageous and provocative music and videos. He's successful and materialistic himself. I'm convinced that he's an intelligent human being, but he seems to have painted himself into a corner. He has to find a new way to shock us with each album, and he's left with the shallowness of shock for its own sake. His public persona won't allow him to grow much as an artist.

Cado defends Manson. He's not a hypocrite, he says, he's a genius whose songs expose the deep, dark truth about how hollow modern life is. He has to use shocking images and lyrics because it's the only way to get at how corrupt our culture is. It's the fact that he's willing to say what no one else will say that makes everyone hate him. He's more than just another guy with a band, he's the guy who has the balls and the smarts to be the Antichrist.

I'm surprised at the show to see that Manson doesn't take himself very seriously onstage. Live, there's an element of self-parody, of irony, that I didn't pick up on listening to the CDs. Midway through the show, after "Lunchbox," a song about turning the tables on schoolhouse bullies by growing up to be famous, Manson grins a huge, toothy grin at the audience and bows slowly from the waist. It's a move straight out of a Bugs Bunny cartoon, and it's funny.

Manson may bill himself as the Antichrist, he may draw, as he did that night, sign-carrying protesters from the Christian right, but to him, his image is a joke.

Onstage, his message isn't that he's the Antichrist. His message is, "See how little it takes to set these morons off?"

IT TAKES MORE THAN an hour to get backstage to see Manson. Finally, we are led to a small room where Manson sits with his bass player, Twiggy Ramirez, and an attractive young woman. Manson is calm, polite, soft-spoken. He's taken his makeup off. He has a glass of an amber liquid in his hand, which I assume is beer. He shakes hands with me, with Cado, with the girl Cado has brought along. There are no drugs in the room, and there's certainly no orgy in progress, nor have we interrupted a satanic ritual. Manson is wearing his trademark contact lens in one eye, which gives that eye a distracting, milky look, almost like he has a cataract, but he insists on sitting on the floor so that I can have a chair.

Manson talks about films and books with my friend. It's his birthday, and he's been to a strip club to celebrate before the show, but it's clear from the way he talks about it that he's gone to the club in search of a kitsch seediness rather than flesh. He talks about his dogs and about a novel he's trying to write. Now that he's offstage, he's pretty ordinary.

Someone knocks on the door, and a woman asks if she can get Mr. Manson anything. He holds his glass up and points.

"I'd love another cream soda," he says.

Cream soda. So that's what the Antichrist drinks.

THESE ARE THINGS I've banned during my son's teenage years: Mohawks, tattoos, piercings outside of the earlobe, sleepovers, Marilyn Manson, skipping school, shoplifting, a black trench coat, smoking pot in his bedroom, binge drinking on our property, staying out all night, the word "fuck" written all over the walls of his room in Sharpie pen.

These are things I've allowed: black fingernail polish, the Mohawk after he got it anyway, lipstick, eye makeup, bondage pants, a fascination with Sid Vicious, cigarette smoking as long as it's not in the house or anywhere I can see, a beer after a hard day's work, dropping out of high school, staying out all night if he calls to let me know, his girlfriend spending the night in his room after her mother committed suicide.

I'm 0 for 12 on the banned items. I did manage to defer the black trench coat for several years, long enough for the shock of Columbine to wear off. Cado's not, so far as I know, a habitual shoplifter. He mostly follows the "no pot smoking in your bedroom" rule. He has many things written on his walls, and the word "fuck" is not prominent among them, but it's there if you look hard enough.

A lot of people would look at these lists and say I'm a failure as a parent.

I count these among my successes: My son is alive. He still talks to me. He has his GED. He still lives at home and has never run away to live on the streets. He's compassionate. He's unfailingly loyal to his friends and quick to offer them help. He knows how to stick with something until he's met his goal. He's a decent human being.

He's flawed, like all of us, but he's not a sociopath.

My kid is all right.

I Think I'm Goin' Out of My Head

Warning:
An American Teenager
Is Loose in Europe

Dave Barry

THE LAST THING I said to my teenage son as I put him on the plane for Europe was: "Don't lose your passport!"

The second-to-last thing I said was: "Don't lose your passport!"

In fact, if you were to analyze all the statements I made to my son in the week before his departure, they'd boil down to: "Don't lose your passport!"

The message I was trying to convey was that he should not lose his passport. Of course, he did not need to be told this. He is a teenage boy, and teenage boys already know everything. When a boy reaches thirteen years of age, the Knowledge Fairy comes around and inserts into his brain all the information in the entire universe. From that point on, he no longer needs any parental guidance. All he needs is parental money.

This is why a teenage boy who has had a driver's license for a total of two hours knows that he can drive 367 miles per hour in heavy traffic while devoting 2 percent of his attention to the actual road and 98 percent to the critical task of adjusting the radio to exactly the right volume setting ("Death Star"). If you criticize him, he'll give you a look of contempt mixed with pity because you are a clueless old dork who was last visited by the Knowledge Fairy in 1873 and your brain has been leaking information ever since.

And so, when I told my son, as he got onto the plane, not to lose his passport, he rolled his eyes in the way that knowledgeable teenagers have rolled their eyes at their parents dating back to when Romeo and Juliet rolled THEIR eyes at THEIR parents for opposing a relationship that turned out really swell except that they wound up fatally stabbing and poisoning themselves.

At this point, you veteran parents are asking: "So, when did your son lose his passport?" The answer is: Before he legally got into Europe. He may have set an Olympic record for passport-losing because apparently his was stolen, along with all of his traveler's checks, while he was on the plane. Don't ask me how this could happen. My son has tried to explain it to me, but I still don't understand because I have a leaky old brain.

All I know is that when the plane landed, my son had no passport and almost no money. Fortunately, the plane landed in Germany, a carefree, laid-back nation that is not a big stickler for paperwork.

Ha ha! I am, of course, kidding. The national sport of Germany is stickling. So my son spent a number of hours trying to convince various authorities that he was a legal human. Meanwhile, back in the United States, unaware of what had happened, I was exchanging increasingly frantic telephone calls with the mother of the boy my son was supposed to meet in the Frankfurt airport, who had reported back to her that my son had not arrived. The mother had suggested several things that her son could do, such as have my son paged or ask an authority, but of course her son scoffed at these ideas because he is also a teenage boy and thus did not need to be told how to find somebody in a large, unfamiliar, foreign airport. He preferred the time-tested technique of wandering around aimlessly. His mother, who also has a daughter, assured me that girls do not act this way.

Eight fun-filled and relaxing hours after his plane landed, my son finally called me, and I nearly bit my tongue off not telling him I Told You So. He told me that the Germans had graciously agreed not to send him back to Miami, which is good because he would probably have ended up in Kuala Lumpur.

He got a new passport the next day, but replacing the traveler's checks was not so simple. I will not name the brand of traveler's checks involved, except to say that it rhymes with "Wisa." As I write these words, my son and I have both been calling the Wisa people for a week, and they still haven't given us a Final Answer on whether they'll replace the checks. It says on the Wisa website that you can "easily get a refund if your cheques are lost or stolen," but in my son's case, it apparently is going to require a vote of the full United Nations. For security and convenience, my son would have been better off carrying his money in the form of live cattle.

But never mind that. The main thing is, he's safely and legally in Europe, where he and his friend will be backpacking around for a month, relying on their common sense. So if there's a war, you'll know why.

Junior Year

Roberta Israeloff

"I'm GOING TO do good in school this year," Jake says. I'm driving
him to his first day of eleventh grade, which falls on his sixteenth
birthday.

"Well," I say.

"Well what?" he asks.

"You're going to do *well* this year. I'm happy to hear you say
that—"

"Don't," Jake says. I haven't begun my new sentence; he hears my
catch-breath.

"Don't what?" I ask.

"Don't say anything else. Just stop right there."

"All I was going to say was—"

"I know what you were going to say. You were going to tell me
how to raise my average, right? Right?"

"Yes," I say. There's no point trying to deny it. We know each
other too well. And we've had this conversation hundreds of times
before. "But *you* brought it up."

"And *you* can't leave well enough alone. That's why I have no
respect for you. Or Dad." He doesn't turn away or slam anything,

but he hardens his eyes. Silently, we watch his friends pull into the parking lot. I've forgotten that this is the year they all learn to drive. Jake behind the wheel. Now there's an image I've done my best to suppress.

"Have a good day," I say, pulling up to the school, hoping he hears the contrition in my voice.

"Whatever," he mumbles, getting out. I sit for a moment watching a girl with five inches of bare midriff slip out of the car ahead of us. Her heels are longer than her skirt. And parked in the middle of her chin is a big gold stud.

YEARS AGO, AT A BUSINESS meeting, I ended up sitting next to a woman who apologized for arriving late by explaining that her sixteen-year-old daughter had woken up with a raging infection in her recently pierced belly button. "She stared me right in the face," this woman said to me, a perfect stranger, "and swore, swore, that the piercing hadn't caused the infection. How old are your children?" she asked. I told her, adding that I had two boys. "Well, they say boys are easier than girls, but I'm not sure that's true," she said. "Regardless, I'm going to give you just one piece of advice, and I suggest you remember it. It's the only thing that will get you through. You have to treat teenagers as if they're temporarily mentally ill."

JAKE WAS SUPPOSED TO BE the good one. The pliable, accommodating, sweet, and considerate one, who didn't punch holes through walls with his fists, who didn't burst out of the house ripping the screen door from its hinges and burn rubber in our tiny driveway backing out into traffic in the midst of a temper tantrum, who didn't stay out till 4:00 AM without a word after promising to call at midnight to apprise us of his plans, who kept track of his supplies and clothing, who didn't lose a hundred-dollar calculator and two winter coats and then chalk it up to a "bad patch." If his older brother, Ben, was mercurial, Jake was optimistic, forgiving, and forbearing, chock-full of equanimity. While Ben believed in his own invincibility and immunity from harm, Jake feared death. Ben rarely met a substance he didn't want to enter into some type of relationship with; Jake hated the taste of alcohol and, after a week of limited experimentation, declared that marijuana wasn't for him. A model teenager.

But not in school. As soon as he hit high school, he began to underachieve in an almost spectacular way. Incomplete homework. Missing labs. Lousy test grades. Term papers handed in late without title pages, with careless spelling errors. "What's going on?" we asked him. He'd been in the gifted program in elementary school, for goodness sake.

"I don't believe in homework," he said. As if homework had the same ontological status as Santa Claus.

For the first two years of high school, we told ourselves that he'd outgrow this slump, that it was a phase. Now it's junior year. Next year, he'll apply to colleges. "We want you to go to a school where you can have the kind of discussions with people that you enjoy, where you'll be with people who have the same kind of spark and energy and native intelligence that you do."

"I'll be fine," he says. "Relax."

. . . .

RELAX. I DON'T RECALL ever saying that to my parents when I was a teenager. Probably that's because I wasn't relaxed. I constantly worried about my school performance. I remember one particular dinnertime conversation during which I informed my father that having a job wasn't nearly as stressful as being a student. He just showed up every day and collected his paycheck, whereas I continually had to perform and be evaluated. There was just no way he could imagine the anxiety.

I don't remember what my father said. For however ridiculous I must have sounded, he shared my basic worldview—in school, one tried as hard as one possibly could. But this gene, which had been transferred so reliably between the generations, appears to have been switched off at the moment that Jake was conceived.

JAKE'S FIRST MIDSEMESTER progress report arrives in the mail before he gets home from school. I open it. "In danger of failing Spanish," it reads. "Should work harder" and "Homework/assignments missing/late" are the other comments.

When I show it to him, he scans the page, balls it up, throws it in the corner, and says, "I'm not going to fail Spanish if that's what you're worried about. She's just saying that to scare you."

"It's working," I say.

"Relax," he says.

"If you just hand in your work, you could raise your average ten points."

"I'm trying," he says. But every day, as far as I can tell, he walks in the house, deposits his backpack next to the desk near the door, and picks it up again on his way out to school in the morning. Sometimes, after dinner, he announces, "I'll go start my homework now." Which means he'll go to his room, play computer games until about eleven, watch *The Daily Show*, and then putter around until midnight.

After thirteen straight years of living with teenagers, I know why God created them—to remind us of the limits of our own power and knowledge. I thought Ben had taught me that. Apparently, all I gained from the experience of raising Ben is that I'd do a better job if by some medical miracle I had to do it again. You learn how to handle the volatile child, and then you get the quiet, defiant one. There are infinite ways to thwart parents.

AT THE END OF DECEMBER, the day Jake receives his report card—his average is seventy-six, way below his potential—we take my mother out to dinner for her birthday. Sitting with Jake in the back seat, she tries to make conversation. She tells him that Elizabeth, Jake's cousin, has a boyfriend. "Do you have a girlfriend?" she asks Jake. I prepare to hear him roll his eyes.

"Well, yeah, I do," he says.

"You *do?*" Driving, I nearly veer off the road.

Her name is Maureen, and she lives on the rich side of town. "Get this," he says. "She has about a 106 average. She's also editor of the school newspaper and president of the honor society."

"And you're the slacker boyfriend?" my husband asks.

Jake grins slowly, his pride awakening. "Yeah, I guess I'm the slacker boyfriend."

"Well, ask her if she can donate ten points from her average to you."

"You know, that's a good idea," Jake says.

"She hates her mother," he adds. "They fight all the time."

"Fight about what?" I ask. "That her average isn't 108?"

"There are other things besides school," Jake says. "I asked her if she wanted to talk to a therapist. It would do her a lot of good."

JAKE AND I SHARE a therapist, a man about eight years older than I am who has worked in a high school for most of his professional life. "What I'm worried about," I explain, "is that Jake seems so unable to act on his own behalf. He says he wants to do well, but then he can't follow through. He can't rally or marshal his resources."

"You know, not everyone is on the same timetable," the therapist says.

"That's easy for you to say," I said. "Your son went where, to Amherst College?"

"Jake can always transfer to Amherst," he says.

"You mean after he gets straight A plusses at the community college, right?"

He laughs. We have an excellent rapport. "What if we put him on Ritalin?" I ask. "You know, for ADD."

"If Jake has ADD, it's only part of the story."

"What's the whole story?"

"You want him to be the person he's not yet ready to be," the therapist says. "Jake's on his own path. He's his own person. He's not thrilled about growing up. And frankly, that doesn't sound so crazy to me."

DURING THE FEBRUARY BREAK, I take Jake for his first driving lesson. Unfortunately for him, he has to learn on a car with a manual transmission since that's all we have. We go to a school parking lot, and I hold my breath as he shifts into first. The car is old, its transmission very touchy. I explain all I can, but in the end, you learn to drive a car with a stick the same way you learn to ride a bike, by feeling your way through. On his first try, Jake shifts into first. Within an hour, he's driving along the perimeter of the parking lot. I study how he learns: He talks to himself as he assimilates new information, makes adjustments, gives himself pep talks, and never gets too frustrated. He couldn't have been a better student. As we drive home, I say, "If only—"

"Will you just quit it?" he explodes.

"Quit what?" I ask.

"You always bring everything back to school. No matter what I say. I could be talking about elephants in the wild, and you'll find a way to bring it back to school. You have no idea how sick I am of it."

"I didn't say anything," I say.

"You thought it."

"YOU HAVE TO STUDY for the SATs," my husband says. "You can get into a lot of schools if your boards are high, even if your average is a little low. Just take twenty minutes a night. Fifteen. Take ten minutes a night and review vocabulary."

"You know this is going in one ear and out the other," Jake says.

"I HAVE A NEW PLAN," my husband says. It's an early April Saturday morning, and we're walking on the boardwalk at the beach. The day before, we received Jake's SAT scores, which were decent but not great. His latest progress report indicated that he was in danger of failing music. "I'm going to offer him a thousand dollars if he gets his average above 90."

"You can't do that," I say. "You can't bribe a kid. It's the worst thing; all the experts say you can't. He'll work for the money, not for the grades. He won't learn to do things for pleasure, but only for the reward."

"It's our only hope," my husband says.

DURING SPRING BREAK, Jake tells us that he broke up with his girl-friend. "What happened?" we ask. I'm afraid that she broke up with him, as the last one had.

But no, he assures me, he was the instigator. "She was just so bor-ing. I mean, we couldn't have an interesting conversation. All she did was, like, study."

JAKE COMES OUT of school one afternoon beaming. "You know that big English project? On *Macbeth*? Well, I aced it. I got a ninety-nine. It was the highest mark in the class."

"What big project?" I ask.

"I thought I told you about it," he says.

"When did you even work on it?" I ask.

"I have my ways," he says.

"I only hope," I begin, not believing the words that are about to come out of my mouth, "that I'm alive when you have a child in high school, a child who's as bright as you with the same average as you. I'd love to eavesdrop on the conversations you have with him."

"I'm not going to have conversations with him," Jake says. "I'm just going to shrug and say, 'Oh, well.'"

"Oh, well?"

"Yeah, 'Oh, well.'"

"Well, I'm going right home to write that down," I say. "I want to have this in writing. I want to be able to refer to this in the future."

"No problem," Jake says.

DRIVING TO SCHOOL one June morning, now that he has his permit, Jake puts on the radio tuned to the classical station, and a Mozart piano sonata fills the car. "Mozart goes with everything," Jake says, explaining how Mozart built on Bach's musical legacy and anticipated Beethoven's. "Did you learn all this in music class?" I ask.

No, Jake says, he learned it on his own. Music class is a waste of time. His final, I know, is in a week. The teacher is holding review sessions. I'm dying to know if Jake is planning to go.

"You know, I have trouble telling Mozart from Haydn," I say.

"Yeah," Jake says, suddenly animated again. "I do, too. But I realized, what you have to do is listen for what Haydn *doesn't* do, and then you know it's him."

"That's exactly right," I say. "You put your finger on the difference between those two composers perfectly." Jake grins.

Later, after dinner, I relate Jake's reflection on Haydn to my husband. "He should pass music on the basis of that comment alone," I say.

"He should get into college on the basis of that comment," my husband says, "but unfortunately, I don't think it works that way."

"Maybe it should," I say. "I mean, did we ever stop to think that maybe Jake's right? Maybe he knows that he'll turn out fine and we're worrying for nothing. Maybe we're just idiots wasting all this time when we should just be enjoying him."

"In other words," my husband says, "he's the Zen master, and we're the ones who are mentally ill."

"Something like that," I say. We stop to consider this. And the more we relax, the righter it sounds.

The Seven Circles of Hormone Hell

Irene Hopkins

NATURE IS SUPPOSED to be perfect, right? So whose idea was it for mothers to go through menopause just about the time their children are deep in the throes of the teenage years? Teenagers and menopausal women are probably the most hormone-ridden beings known in the natural world. "Mood Swings R Us" could be the name of a store carrying products to help with these two intense transitions in our lives.

I'm forty-eight years old, and as much as I hate to admit it, I am in the time they call the "change of life"—the one characterized by dark moods and shocking moments of disbelief in front of the mirror. It used to be that my hormonal "episodes" came once in a great while. Just a wave now and then. But lately the waves are coming closer together, and there are days when I feel like one is going to wash me away. There's nothing I can do but just wait it out.

I was at my yoga class recently when, toward the end of class, a student asked the teacher if she knew any good poses or yogic ways to counteract the effects of menopause. There was a slight beat, and I couldn't resist filling it with the notion that if she did possess some secret to help women during this time, she would not be our yoga teacher. She would be a very wealthy woman, living on a remote island in an undisclosed location.

Complicating matters is the fact that my daughters are going through their own hormonal adjustments, and the combination can be deadly. At the very least, it can seriously threaten family harmony. And the truth is, there is really nothing that eliminates the effects on either end of the spectrum.

On a recent summer morning, I woke up with a familiar heavy feeling. I dragged my body out of bed to get ready for work. Every movement felt like I was wading through a lake of molasses. I stared at the clothes in my closet for about ten minutes, hating everything. I finally chose an outfit, even though it made me feel fat and dowdy. Hair and makeup, whatever. I trudged downstairs to the kitchen, where my husband was reading the newspaper, all showered and ready for the world. I poured hot water into my teacup and began stirring a little honey into it. Something about that made me sad. I could feel the tears welling in my eyes. I looked at my husband, and he looked back with confusion, then concern, and then, finally, recognition. You see, over the last few years, he has become an expert at recognizing the signs, too. Tears flowing, I nodded and choked out the word, although it wasn't really necessary: "hormones."

I slogged my way through work, doing my best not to impose my bleak mood on my coworkers. What kept me going was the thought of home, the couch, and some really good, dark chocolate.

My teenage girls, whom I had left sleeping in summer vacation bliss, would be up by now. Surely one of them would understand and give me a foot massage.

The car ride home was encouraging. Brilliant sunshine, the sweet smell of summer in the air. I turned on the radio. Joni Mitchell. "Sittin' in a park in Paris, Fra-ance . . ." Her voice sounded impossibly young, singing familiar lines that reminded me of a time, not so long ago, when I was young and carefree, traveling in Europe and unencumbered by the trappings of middle age. I started crying anew.

Home at last. I walked in the front door to the sound of rap music blasting from the back room. My younger daughter was in the bathroom working the flat iron and hair dryer to death. "Hi, honey," I greeted her. She spun around. Her eyes sent sparks of anger in my direction. "My hair looks awful today. I hate it. I hate my hair." (She was on top of the world just yesterday *because* of her beautiful new haircut.) "Can I help?" I asked weakly. "No," she snapped, and stormed past me, because apparently this was my fault.

I followed her upstairs and headed to my older daughter's room to say hello, still hoping for that foot massage. My eldest sat in the middle of her room crying, surrounded by what seemed like every item of clothing she owned. "What's wrong?" I asked.

"I have nothing to wear. I have no clothes. And I have no friends."

What happened to all the friends she had yesterday? I wondered to myself. "What do you mean, you have no friends?" I asked, mustering up as much sympathy as I could.

"There's just no one," she said hopelessly, pulling a stray shoe out from underneath her and flinging it at the wall. "Everyone is busy. Everyone has a boyfriend. I just can't find anyone who I can connect with. And I hate my school."

There were times when I could sit down and reason with her. We'd go through her clothes and see that she actually did have plenty to wear. Or maybe we'd make plans to go shopping and find a few new things. But this was not one of those times. My coping skills were low, and I knew that if I tried to help, I would only make it worse. For example, I could have pointed out that she does have friends, wonderful friends. And that if she would put some of these clothes away, she'd find that she has more clothes than most people in the world (reminding me of my mother's "starving children in Biafra" line—not gonna go there). Or worse, I might have even segued into how *I'm* feeling, how she's not the *only one* with problems today. Instead, I just turned and left the room. It was better that way. I passed my younger daughter, still fretting over her hair, and headed for my own room. And there we were. Three hormonal females in the same house—polarized by the intense, negative energy emanating from our awful beings.

I grew up in a family of seven siblings, five of whom were girls. There was a time when we were all menstruating, and, as women often do, all at the same time. We had an entire closet devoted to Kotex—our own modern-day version of the red tent. My poor brothers and father. When my mother was going through her change—which wasn't pretty—she blurted out on one especially difficult day, "I just hope I live long enough to see one of you have a teenager." Well, here I am, with two of them.

When my older daughter first started her period, she pointed out that we were on opposite ends of the spectrum, going through a beginning and an end together. It was a lovely and profound thought for a girl of eleven, and I cherished our newly found sisterhood. I explained about hormones, held her when she cried for no reason, and taught her the tricks of the trade, including how to take special care of herself during the hardest days. She began to sympathize with me when I had cramps, and it was good to have someone in the house with true, experiential simpatico. But it was early—for both of us.

Three years later, with things beginning to heat up on my end of the spectrum, the situation took a turn for the worse. By now we were pretty much in sync, cyclically speaking, so my husband and younger daughter learned to stay out of our way for a few days of each month. But even on the best of days, there were other issues that wreaked havoc with our individual hormonal imbalances. Her room started to look like an "after the earthquake" simulation, and she began responding to any suggestion that we do something as a family as if we had asked her to clean the garage floor. With her tongue. And yet, she cried for independence. She wanted her driver's license. She was yearning to be free, and she was ready, she claimed, to live on her own.

Fast-forward to the present. My younger daughter is now thirteen and on the brink. We're starting all over again. But this time, there's something else going on. I call it the nerd factor. Mine, not my daughters'. I'm becoming painfully aware of my aging body, my uncool clothes, and, in the eyes of my younger daughter, my total inability to dance or sing. I can actually embarrass her when there is no one in the room but the two of us. God forbid I do something in public.

Not long after that miserable, hormonally charged afternoon, the whole family went to my sister's annual solstice party. It was a hot summer night, the DJ was playing cool music, and I was feeling *gooood*. A string of songs from college days brought a bunch of us to our feet, dancing and remembering. I felt young and comfortable with my body, and I was laughing and enjoying myself along with the others on the dance floor. Suddenly, my thirteen-year-old appeared. She was passing through the crowd with a few of her compadres dressed in their best middle school chic, some carrying skateboards, heading en masse for the soda cooler. My daughter spotted me dancing, stopped in her tracks, and looked at me like I was a living faux pas. With eyes rolled back so far in her head I wondered if she could see, she turned and walked away as quickly as possible before any of her friends saw the spectacle.

Sometimes I am able to laugh at these moments. But there are times when I find myself crumbling inside as I struggle with the changes I see in the mirror. Much has been written about the time of life that I am entering—a time when wisdom replaces youthful beauty. Women in their menopausal years are revered and honored in certain cultures for their all-encompassing womanhood. Unfortunately, our culture fights age relentlessly and aggressively, making it difficult to accept what nature is handing us. "Desiderata" reminds us that we should "age gracefully, surrendering the things of youth." Although I am determined to embrace my progress into wisdom and wholeness, it's hard to surrender. And it isn't always so graceful.

When I walk down the street with my daughters, the males we pass are now looking at them with appreciation, and no longer at me. My girls are blossoming with beauty, fresh and clean and so very lovely. When I look at them I feel happy for them—and proud. But they do provide a stark contrast for what is happening to me. I wonder if without them I'd notice my own changes to quite the same degree. Would my skin look as loose, would my hair look as dull, would my waist look as thick if I were not standing beside my daughters? I'm not jealous of them. But I have to adjust as I pass the torch. It seems so all of a sudden, all of a sudden.

The other day, I was in the car at a red light when I thought about my older daughter leaving for college next year and my younger one, my baby, already looking toward high school. I was overcome with emotion and shock at how little time we have left. I will miss them both terribly. But when the nest is finally empty, maybe my emotional state will be in a place where I can rejoice, not mourn. Not so much at their absence—the house will seem awfully big and quiet without them and all their stuff—but at the knowledge that we made it, that I did my job, that my daughters are on their own and doing well.

Come to think of it, without all these hormonal changes, my daughters and I might still be blissfully thinking of each other as perfect creatures. We'd gaze adoringly at each other over frothy lattes, go for long walks together, and get our nails done. The Queen of Cool and her two adoring daughters. I would never want them to leave. I would have to homeschool them through the college years.

Hmmm.

Maybe there is something to this menopause-meets-adolescence. Maybe it's what makes it possible for me to say goodbye without the awful sting I once anticipated.

Maybe nature is perfect after all.

Sex Education

Nancy Blakey

·

As THE MOTHER of four children and a self-declared eternal optimist, I've spent twenty years helping other parents and children find joy in their family lives. From the time my children were small, I began writing books aimed at creating family fun and encouraging parent-child bonds. I became an expert on parent education, presenting workshops on how we can bring our best selves to our lives as parents. What better career for someone who loves to communicate, doodle, and hum than to teach others to do the same with their families?

"You can't push rewind on childhood" is one of my favorite tenets, delivered to audiences with authority. And, for the most part, I have lived my mothering years with this conviction—full-throttle appreciation for every moment and few regrets. But if I were ever given the chance to rewind, erase one scene, and do it over, I know exactly which moment I would choose.

Our firstborn, Jenna, was everything a parent could possibly dream of: a black-eyed, gorgeous child who was smart, generous, and wise beyond her years. Soon after her birth, my husband, Greg, and I had three boys in quick succession. Greg fished in Alaska several months out of the year, so I was often single-handedly raising a tribe of children under the age of five. Four children and me. Believe it or not, I loved it.

Because of her firstborn status, Jenna became my right hand, especially during my annual stints of single mothering. She grew up helping to shepherd her brothers through the obstacle courses of childhood, earning money during summers in Alaska by working the slime line gutting fish, and riding horses in her free time. Over the years, she has been called stubborn, a charmer, a pistol, a beauty. I often called her a handful, but in the best sense of the word: a handful of self-possession, knowing her mind, intuitively understanding what was needed next.

Oh, I had my ideas of what was needed next as my firstborn progressed from childhood to adolescence. But as a parent educator, I also knew it was best to raise children to heed their authentic selves. More than anything, I wanted Jenna to withstand the pressure of what others thought and claim the world for herself.

I began talking to Jenna and her brothers about sex when they were young. I was fearless that way. It was easy to start their education when we joined Greg up in Alaska for the sockeye salmon season. "See? The female salmon lay those eggs, and then the males spray sperm on top to fertilize them. That's how you get baby fish!"

It was a concrete and effective beginning to sex, if from a fish perspective. While the younger ones wandered off to look for fossils and feathers, Jenna always wanted to know more. I would go as far as she would take me. *How does it happen for people?* She asked. *Where do your eggs come from? How does the baby come out?* I answered everything straight and true. We delivered lambs and poked the afterbirth.

Given my commitment to communication, it's not surprising that we talked about everything so intimately—changing bodies, periods, and boys. When her body began to mature, I told her she would know when she was ready for sex. That it would be a long, long time. That she needed to be in a loving, committed relationship with someone who would support any decision she made. And it had to be *her* choice, no one else's. *Resist pressure!* I exhorted. *You are special!*

Jenna was fourteen years old when she met her first love, Sam. He was sixteen, handsome, and shy, and he loved Jenna with all his tender heart. She was in heaven. She had her fierce horse to ride in the afternoons and a boyfriend who kissed her and told her she was beautiful and made her laugh that tickly musical laugh of hers that meant trouble. That meant come-hither. That she used on her brothers when she hatched trickery. I knew it well, but was unsure of what it meant with Sam.

Ah, Sam. I really liked him. He made eye contact and hung out with us. He enjoyed Jenna's younger brothers, helped with the dishes, and made a new seat for the swing when he broke the old one. Jenna and Sam were together for two years. It was a peaceful relationship.

Truth be told, I can't exactly remember how much Jenna and I talked about sex during that time. I wish I could say frequently, that it was a natural and inclusive dialogue between us, but that would be a lie. We talked about everything and everyone else. Body image, goals, horse dreams, relationship dilemmas, and, among other things, which of her friends were being pressured to have sex.

"I'm certainly not!" she exclaimed. "I am in control of my relationship with Sam. Don't worry, he never pushes me past my comfort zone."

I left those conversations feeling relieved. Dare I say it? Self-congratulatory. Our bond was so tight; of course she would tell me if she and Sam were even thinking about having sex. Of course I would know when she became sexually active. And of course she would wait. A long, long time.

One weekend, a friend visited from the East Coast. Now, Maia is one hip and happening mama. An actress, she started a play company in Manhattan and raised two strong children. I love her. I value her opinion. When she asked about the kids, I told her about Sam as part of the overall snapshot. Maia made an offhand comment about how she was sure a girl like Jenna would be smart about birth control. "She doesn't need it," I told her. Maia smiled and took my hand. "How long have they been together?" she asked. I swallowed hard. The moment I was alone, I marched upstairs and knocked on Jenna's bedroom door. She was sitting cross-legged on the floor, knotting hemp cords into a necklace. She looked up serenely and said hi.

"Jenna, I have a question." The words sounded exactly like *I have a gun.*

"What is it?" she asked, alarmed.

"Are you and Sam sexually active?"

Jenna smiled and looked down at her hands. "Why do you ask?"

The question stung me with its sideways implication. Suddenly, I wanted to hurt her with tiny arrows of my own shock. I wanted her to feel my pain.

"Yes, Mom, we are," Jenna said defiantly. "I have been wanting to tell you for some time. I just didn't know how."

I felt the inner gate that edits thoughts before they issue from my mouth bust open and swing wildly on its hinges. I howled. I screamed. I wept. I will not write down the things I said because no one should have to read the primal storm that I spewed. Suffice to say, it was along the lines of *How could you be so stupid? You idiot, you've ruined your life, have you learned nothing?* Etc., etc., miserable, etc. Jenna flared back indignantly.

"It's everything you asked!" she shouted. "We are in a committed relationship! We waited! I knew I was ready! I was not pressured! IT WAS MY IDEA!"

I ran sobbing from her room and slammed the door. I groped my way to our bedroom and slammed that door, too, just in case Jenna didn't know how upset I was. Greg was shaving in the bathroom and looked up.

"What was that all about?" he asked, rinsing the razor.

"Greg, Jenna is sexually active."

I paused to let the words sink in and hit him hard like they hit me. He made that man-shaving face in the mirror and slid the razor across his cheek.

"And?" he said.

"What do you mean AND?" I cried. "Did you hear me? She is having SEX with SAM!"

Greg set the razor down gently and held me by the shoulders.

"Nancy, Nancy, Nancy. What did you expect? I'd be surprised if they weren't. They've been together two years. Sam is eighteen. They love each other. I met you when I was eighteen, remember?"

Struggling out of his hold, I screamed a terrible version of *Some father you are.* Greg went back to shaving. Jenna was silent behind her door.

I threw myself on the bed and stared at the ceiling, my world fractured and reeling. Like a car accident, or unexpectedly falling downstairs, it was the surprise as much as the event itself that cut deep. Somehow, over the years, the pleasant, irrational convictions that Jenna and I would be close forever, that she would tell me all her secrets, that I would help to extricate her from predicaments, had built an architecture of sureness on which I hung our relationship. I was blindsided by my own blindness.

The rest of Maia's visit was a blur. I know I cooked, we drank wine, we went for a hike in the Olympics. Jenna came with us. The brain does strange things in the vise grip of agony. I struggled to stay ahead of her on the steep and narrow trail out of a twisted logic that went something like this: If I fall behind, all will be lost. I will forever limp slowly behind my vigorous children, growing older and feebler as they forge nimbly ahead. I concentrated on putting one foot in front of the other as fast as I could. That is all I remember.

Over the next week, even my best self-soothing techniques failed. The ones I used when my dad died or when I was overwhelmed with responsibilities. I crooned to myself: *Of course you would choose a passionate, strong daughter over a meek and mild one any day.*

Wrong, I thought with a snort. *I could do with meek and mild right now.*

I tried reasoning with myself: Nothing had changed from a week ago except a small piece of information that told me Jenna was right. She was in a committed relationship, they love each other, there was no pressure, and she waited. *Well, then, why couldn't she have waited a few more years?*

And then a small, unbidden thought surfaced: *Since when did age, or anything, or anyone, stop you from doing what you felt needed to be done?* It was that thought that finally helped me turn down the volume and dwell in the unfamiliar silence between my daughter and me.

In that silence, the educator in me remembered: There are a thousand ways to raise a happy and healthy child. I have seen strict parents and lenient parents do it. I have watched intact families, single parents, rich and poor manage to instill a sense of purpose and meaning in their children. There is no grand formula, no one set of criteria for success save one: There is a sense of relationship between parent and child. However misguided, lopsided, or messy the connection may be, if there is a relationship, there is hope, there is forgiveness, there is a certain elasticity that absorbs the lurches of mistakes and failure.

In the end, it was our relationship that saved us—our mutual need for the other to be sound, to be whole, to work and play side by side again with casual indifference. We missed that lovely carelessness with every act, every chore, and every conversation. Our yearning for its return was so great that I began to forget my pain, and I would lean into her as we drove to the barn, or I would touch the back of her neck with my hand as she bent to her home-work. Jenna leaned back, she looked into my eyes, and I found myself apologizing. Not convincingly at first, but it was a start.

Later, I told her my anger is always fear in disguise. It seems safer to slash and burn and rage my way through fear than to cry or become silent. I was worried about sexually transmitted diseases and pregnancy. I was fearful of her vulnerability, my loss of control, the role that sexuality can play in a young girl's life in subordinating her needs and ambition to the linking of her arm through a boy's. Jenna said she was afraid to tell me because we *were* close, and, anticipat-ing a less-than-happy response, she didn't want to drive a wedge between us. Did I understand? The educator in me understood. The mother unwillingly grieved.

We cobbled out a truce, the beginning of a new relationship that felt complicated with new rules. Would it always be this way? Jenna returned to the solace of her horse. I returned to the mothering of her brothers, their needs met with peanut butter and more wood for the fort they were building.

One afternoon, I arrived early at the barn and leaned on the fence as Jenna and her thoroughbred, Madison, approached the final jump of the day. At the last possible second, he refused it, and Jenna flew over his head, crashed into the jump, and landed heavily on her back in the dirt. My chest pounded as I ran to her.

"I'm okay, I'm okay ..." she said, waving me off. She drew a deep breath, got to her feet, and told me to step back. I stood at the fence railing as Jenna pulled herself onto Madison, made several passes around the arena, and then faced the jump one more time. I held my breath as they sailed over and landed perfectly. Jenna grinned as she triumphantly patted Madison's sweaty neck.

And suddenly I saw that the motion of regaining my seat hadn't been enough with Jenna. I was still holding back. I needed to haul up my strength, my heart, and steadfast conviction that our relationship would heal and renew. The poet Robert Frost once said the best way out is always through. Jenna, my right hand, was showing me the way. Now it was time to follow her lead.

"Mom? Everything's okay, but . . ."

Linda Rue Quinn

I'M GOING TO FORM a support group. "Parents of Teenagers" or "POT" for short. We'll even set up a hotline for those times when your teenager seems suicidal because he keeps doing things that he knows will make you want to strangle him. 1-800-HELP-ME.

This number could also be used for those questions that are always in the back of my mind, such as "Does a black hole really exist in my daughter's bedroom?" or "Why do we keep finding the hand soap in her room?" We don't ask her anymore. We just give her a strange look as we take the hand soap and return it to its home, knowing it will end up back in her room for some secret governmental science project that she's working on.

Maybe the hotline could be used to answer questions about how to get the stains out of her carpet. So far, the list includes red and orange paint, corn syrup, blue food dye, fingernail polish and remover, and let's not forget the soot stain leading to her balcony door from the fire.

Fire, you ask? Oh, that's another story.

Perhaps to celebrate our anniversary, my son set the second-story balcony on fire. Not on purpose, mind you, but still, it burned. It was my second week on a new job, and I get a phone call from my son.

"Mom?" he says. "Everything's okay."

I've lived with him long enough to know it isn't.

"We put the fire out," he continues.

I sit down hard at my desk and try to breathe.

"I accidentally set the balcony on fire."

Of course that makes everything okay, because it wasn't intentional. I find my voice.

"Is it out?"

"Yes."

"Are you sure?"

"Yes, Mom."

"What happened?"

"Well, I was playing around with candles."

"Candles?"

"Yes, but I got Grandma out . . . "

"Are you sure it's out?"

"Yes, Cindy put it out with the hose after I jumped off the balcony and ran in to get Grandma out of the house."

"What?" Brain overload. Circuits breaking.

"Grandma was in the bathroom, and I told her the house was on fire and we needed to get out first while Cindy was calling 911."

"911? Did they come?"

"No, Cindy called to cancel after we put the fire out."

"Are you sure it's out?"

"Mom . . . " Now he's trying not to sound annoyed, because even he knows this is not the time.

"What did Grandma do?"

"She didn't want to come outside because she was in her night-gown, but when I told her the house might burn down, she let me help her out."

"Okay, so that's the first good thing I've heard. You used your head. But . . . wait a minute, how did you say this happened? What were you doing with candles?"

"Well, I was doing an experiment."

"With candles?"

"And gas."

"Gas?"

"Mower gas. And oil."

Over the next few days, I asked him several times, "What were you thinking? I just want to know your thought process. I want to know every step behind you actually going to the shed to get this flammable material to play around with on the *balcony*."

He kept saying, "I don't know what I was thinking."

So I responded each time, "Son, if at any time you don't know what you're thinking, please stop what you're doing immediately. Promise me."

After I arrived home that afternoon and surveyed the damage, I decided to risk going out for our anniversary dinner. I called my husband at work and told him about the whole mess, then drove to meet him at our favorite restaurant. I drink alcohol maybe once or twice a year. When I walked into the restaurant, he had a drink waiting for me. I love this man.

Every day when I call home, I ask my son, "Have you set anything on fire?" He used to be offended, but sometimes he even calls me with the news. "Guess what, Mom? I didn't set anything on fire today."

Now about that support group . . .

The Accidental Boy Scout

Peter Applebome

AT FIRST, I ASSUMED it was a passing phase, like the Teenage Mutant Ninja Turtles or Mighty Morphin Power Rangers.

After all, the only credible template we have for our kids' teenage years is what happened to us—in my case, it was a cross between *Leave It to Beaver* and *The Strawberry Statement* that provided me various hazy scenarios for adolescent glory or ruin, most of them having to do with sports, music, Salingerian alienation, and girls who didn't know I was alive.

None of these scenarios had anything to do with the absence of indoor plumbing. None included internal-frame backpacks, outback ovens, or four-season tents with front and rear vestibules. None in any shape, manner, or form touched on the tying of knots, the collective contemplation of farts, the swearing of sacred oaths, or the participation in camporees, trekorees, jamborees, or Klondike derbies. In none of them was I forced to ponder the question: What do you do if you see an endangered animal eating an endangered plant? In short, were I to have spent weeks in the academic exercise of imagining the course of my son's teenage years, I would never have come up with what happened. Green hair or bad poetry, maybe. Obsessions with box scores and draft picks, probably. Whatever his generation's version of the Beatles, Stones, Byrds, and Dylan turned out to be, almost certainly. The Boy Scouts? *The Boy Scouts?* Do what?

But, as every parent learns, we only think we get to write the script. So after waiting, and waiting and waiting, for this strange and unexpected detour to pass, I decided to come along. To my utter surprise, I was soon sucked in. We expect our kids to lead us into some inscrutable future, and it's one of the many conceits of the geezer/boomer cohort that we assume their future will be somehow cooler, edgier, more knowing, more out-there than ours was. In short, just like ours only with better hair, a less pompously messianic vision of their place in the political cosmos, and updated for iPods, Blackberries, hip-hop, instant messaging, Napster, downloads, cell phones that take your picture, and other things I still haven't figured out. But, of course, if the path were that clear, generational change would unfold like some interstate knifing in a straight line through the desert rather than the jerry-rigged blue highway zig-zag it more commonly turns out to be. So, rather than a hip trip to the future, my son led me back to some moldy cultural dinosaur, something I never did for a second as a kid or considered for a second as an adult. I'll be eternally grateful that he did.

(Political Disclaimer: I think the Boy Scouts are wrong in a big way on their policy of banning gays from being Scoutmasters. So, it turns out, does our Scoutmaster, who drafted an antidiscrimination mission statement for the troop. But I also think it's a mistake to let one issue define Scouting or for liberals to cede yet another iconic piece of America to the right. If that's not good enough for you, either because you think the policy is correct or you think all right-thinking dads have a moral duty to pull their kids out, you might as well just quit here and go on to the next essay.)

First stop was a Cub Scout troop in Atlanta. Ben would pore over his Wolf Cub Scout Book, Big Bear Cub Scout Book, and Webelos Scout Book and ask questions I was ill equipped to answer about first aid, animal tracks, or camping gear. But, to be honest, I barely noticed. I was willing—no, delighted—to skip a work trip to the White House to make it to a big Little League playoff game, or to play basketball or baseball on the driveway or front lawn with his friends for as long as they could stand it. But picking him up at his Scout meetings seemed about all the commitment I was ready for in that particular sphere. I'm not sure which appealed to me less, Scouting's military trappings and Dudley Do-Right image or the prospect of horrid and pointless excursions into a realm of dubious cuisine, sanitation, and creature comforts. Did I mention indoor plumbing? My view was: Fine for him, as long as it lasts, but on this one, I'll take a pass.

And then that was no longer good enough. When Ben was ready to enter middle school, we moved to suburban New York, a development that in the parenting environment of the time seemed fraught with incalculable peril. What kind of a monster uproots his kids from their happy home just because he needs to keep his job? I could already see the headlines fifteen years hence: "Serial Killer Was Normal Until Family Was Uprooted. Would Never Have

Snapped Had He Not Moved, Friends and Neighbors Confirm. Top Leading Experts Blame Dad for Slaying Spree." So, facing the stigma and eternal damnation of being judged a Bad Dad, I not only made sure he found a new troop, but figured I'd come along for an excursion or two as a gesture of goodwill and paternal contrition.

Our first outing with Troop 1 Chappaqua was a canoe trip on the Delaware River, where our Scoutmaster, Dr. Flank, proceeded to strike terror into our hearts before we even put a paddle in the water. He reminded us of the risk of hypothermia—a recurring theme, we soon learned—if we capsized in the fifty-degree waters, the prospect of drowning if our feet got caught on underwater boulders, and how getting stuck on a rock could bring another doomsday scenario as our canoe filled instantly with a half ton of water. We listened intently, shoved off, and within ten seconds found ourselves stuck on the first rock we saw—or, more accurately, didn't see. As I waited for the half ton of water to engulf us, it occurred to me that if I drowned Ben and myself in our first ten seconds of a Scouting activity, I would go down in history as the single worst Scout who ever lived. As things turned out, we managed to shimmy the canoe off the rock and narrowly evade the Reaper. Then, perhaps energized by the exhilaration of our near-death experience, we ended up having quite a gala day as part of a flotilla of Scouts and dads lazing down the river and navigating its very modest rapids on a perfect September afternoon. We drove back infused with the identical jolt of energy, excitement, and discovery.

Next came our first camping trip. We had borrowed a friend's tent, an item I had never seen any possible use for until now, and

I had managed to put it up in the living room in advance of our excursion into the wilderness. But once we got there, my tiny measure of competence disappeared. Which side needed the long pole, and which needed the short one? What's the point of the rain fly, and can't we just forget it? I did my best to project a modicum of paternal self-assurance, but I wasn't fooling anyone. Finally, Mr. Johnson, one of Dr. Flank's able assistants, wandered over, rolled his eyes, and set it up for us.

"You got your bear bag?" he then asked.

"Our WHAT?" I blurted out in a voice that no doubt betrayed more concern than I wanted to express at that moment.

"Your BEAR BAG," he responded twice as loud, the way Americans do in foreign countries when they assume the ignorant locals will understand their English if they just say it loud enough.

"Holy shit," I thought. Surely the chances of a bear wandering into our campsite were quite small, but even so, if we were expected to trap a bear in some kind of bag, shouldn't we have had just a bit of preparation? Questions began racing through my brain. What kind of bag could it possibly be? Where did you get one? Did you sneak up behind the bear and slip the bag over him? Or did you set a trap—presumably with a honey jar—and wait for him to wander into the bear bag? What if the bear didn't fit in the bear bag? Shouldn't we have had some bear-bag instruction rather than on-the-job training with one thousand pounds of very hacked-off bear? What if he got out? What if he didn't get out? Where could you possibly take a bear bag loaded, as it were, for bear? What did loaded for bear mean, anyway? Which was the really mean one, the black bear or the brown bear? And would it matter much if you had an angry bear already in your bear bag? Wouldn't either be mean enough?

"You hang it from a tree, Dad," said Ben patiently, realizing the nature, if not the extent, of my confusion. "You put your food in a bag and hang it from a tree so the bears can't get it. Bears have a great sense of smell, so you don't want any food in your tent. It's very unlikely there's a bear around, but you do it just in case."

Oh. *That* bear bag. As Emily Litella used to say, "Never mind."

We had many other experiences, wonderful and wretched, in the next three years. There was a transcendent hike up Hunter Mountain one fall: We began on a crisp October morning and hiked up the mountain until we arrived at a pristine, snow-covered peak. It felt as if we had journeyed not from one place but from one season to another, like the ultimate metaphor for change and transformation. There was a nightmarish canoe trip in a nonstop monsoon where the kids started turning blue and we had to abort the mission before Dr. Flank's warnings about hypothermia finally came true. There was the canoe trip (there were lots of canoe trips) where the damn thing finally did capsize, leaving us feeling not just soaked but stupid. There were three—count 'em, three—one-week stints in which I served as a poor imitation of an assistant Scoutmaster at beautiful Camp Waubeeka at the Curtis S. Read Scout Reservation in the Adirondacks. There was also, however, my one shining moment of Scouting Greatness at the end of the third, when, under my tutelage, the troop won the coveted Waubeeka Award for General Excellence and I won the Scoutmaster Challenge—the single most undeserved honor since Athenians started handing out laurel wreaths.

Still, through it all, there were certain constants. We were operating on Ben's turf, not on mine. Particularly as time went by, we depended on his competence and knowledge, not, thankfully, on my paltry skills. He got to know all the dads who came along, and I got to know all the kids, so the experience played out in a shared community with its Chaucerian array of heroes and knaves. And it was truly a shared experience, in which we took the same trips, ate the same chili and spaghetti, slept in the same tent, and listened to the same ghost stories around the campfire at night.

I'm not going to claim that Everything I Know About Parenting I Learned in the Boy Scouts, but they do a few things right in a big way. They're right on the way both dads and kids grow by sharing the same experiences. There's enormous value in the way the process unfolds over a long period of time, so you watch not just your kid but the rest of the posse grow up from incorrigible goofballs to quite competent young men. It's one of the few ways that a dad gets to share the experience of his son's maturation with other dads going through the same thing. And, current politics aside, the core Scout values—a Scout is trustworthy, loyal, helpful, friendly, courteous, kind, obedient, cheerful, thrifty, brave, clean, and reverent—are as important for the dads to remember as they are for the kids to learn. You can get some of those things in places far cooler than the Boy Scouts, but I'm not sure most of us ever do.

Scouting didn't begin as my world, and it didn't end up that way, either. If I never again have to wake up on a frigid morning and stumble through the woods to go to the bathroom, that will be just fine, thanks. But you're not a parent for very long, particularly in that twilight zone where, without you even realizing it, your relationship with your son changes from one thing to another, like our magical climb up Hunter Mountain.

I hope I led Ben in some good directions, but our adventures with our friends and coconspirators in Troop 1 turned out to be one rich, revealing, totally unexpected way that he has led me, even if he could lead me only so far. On spring and summer nights when I get off the train, the field by the station is usually full of other dads' kids playing Little League games in the dwindling sunlight or under the lights at the Rec Department field. I sometimes stop and watch for a few minutes, taking in the busy green pageant and listening to the chatter of the kids, the *ping* of the balls flying off the metal bats, and the familiar *thud* of ball meeting glove. Invariably, I get a wistful pang of remembrance and regret. How did that end so fast?

We don't get out with the troop all that much these days. Ben's busy with school, other diversions, and the anxiety-ridden Olympus of suburban life, applying to college. We keep meaning to make more of the trips with the troop, but somehow it usually doesn't happen, and now there's a whole crop of eager new kids who seem impossibly young, the way Ben did when we first ventured down this path. Part of me will be perfectly happy never to set foot in a tent again. But most of me looks back on our journeys into the outback with our goofy little posse of kids and dads every bit as fondly as I remember every season with the Giants, Braves, or Mets. And I know I'll get a similar shiver of remembrance and regret when this is over, too.

How to Get into College
Without Really Trying

Gail Hudson

SEPTEMBER

When my daughter was younger, I hated it when parents would say to me in an ominous tone, "Just wait until she becomes a teenager." But today I heard myself using that exact same voice with an innocent mother of a middle-schooler. "Just wait until she starts applying to college."

The general rule of advice for parents of high school seniors is this: Let the students run this show; give them the responsibility to make it happen. Our role as parents is simply to be their support staff.

As far as I can tell, my daughter's version of "running the show" means avoiding all discussion of college applications. "I'm too tired to talk about it now," she tells me on her way upstairs for a shower. Or, "I'm too busy, can we do this later?" as she heads into a corner of the house to practice piano. The problem is she is tired, or busy, all of the time.

. . . .

SENIORS DON'T WANT their parents taking over the application process. At least that's what the college advisor I hired tells me when I called her today. That's right, I hired a college advisor. Gabrielle goes to a public high school of sixteen hundred students, with four hundred students per guidance counselor. For $100 an hour, I hired someone to do what my child won't let me do and the high school guidance counselor doesn't have time to do—go over all of my daughter's academic and social interests, research the schools that match those interests, then make a reasonable list of choices.

I also thought a college advisor would give her a little bit of an edge. The first time we met with the college advisor, in fact, was just after my daughter finished her sophomore year.

"This is a little early," she told me. "Most parents start talking with me toward the end of the junior year."

I felt embarrassed by my display of anxiety, but also relieved that Gabrielle was a step ahead of the others.

EVERYONE WANTS TO know where she is applying to college. In certain circles, this list contains an unspoken code: super-high achiever (Ivy League), medium-high achiever (small, private liberal arts), all the way down to slacker (local community college).

I realize this is elitist and superficial, but sometimes I find myself rising to the competitive bait. There I am in the neighborhood video store or the grocery checkout line, name-dropping the schools Gabrielle's considering, all the places we've visited, and hungrily listening to the other students' lists. I hate this about myself, but I can't seem to stop. It's the playground scene all over again: whose kid is walking, whose kid can climb the ladder alone. When will it ever end?

THE COLLEGE ADVISOR insists that I stop making the appointments for my daughter—she can use the phone, she can email, she knows where to find me. You need to let her own this, she tells me. If she can't step into it, maybe she's just not ready to go to college.

I try taking a casual approach. "So how's it going with the college stuff?"

"It's not working," Gabrielle tells me. "Your anxiety is oozing out of every pore in your body. It's contaminating the room."

If I stop holding the anxiety, she will have to hold it. I know this. And yet, holding anxiety is like holding on to control.

It's hard to let go and trust that it's all going to be okay.

OCTOBER

I get a letter from the high school. My daughter has four unexcused absences from her AP art class. Two more absences and she is in danger of getting a grade of NC, the letter states—No Credit. I immediately grab the calculator and tally how this will affect her GPA. Okay, studio art is not a core curriculum grade, but it is what she wants to major in at college. An NC would reduce her GPA an entire tenth of a point. Gabrielle's a National Latin Scholar, her SATs are stellar, but her GPA has been mysteriously slipping lately.

I confront her when she returns from school.

"Come on," she says. "I can't believe you think I would actually fail art." Her face is smudged with charcoal, and she has crusted acrylic paint under her fingernails. "It's just that art is my first class after lunch, and if I'm more than five minutes late, she has to mark it as an absence. You can call her. I never miss a class."

This soothes me. But in the middle of the night, I wake up fuming. Why does she have to be late after lunch? If she screws up this art grade, I will scream my head off at her. I'll make her pay for this.

I make some warm milk. My anger feels all confused.

BEING A PARENT OF a high school senior is like a spiritual practice. Don't attach to the fear. Don't attach to future outcomes. Just be in the now. Sometimes, I can be a little Buddha—knowing that it doesn't really matter where she goes to college. She has straight teeth. She knows how to ride a horse and fast-pitch a softball. She is smart, funny, and creative. She has parents, grandparents, uncles, aunts, cousins, neighbors, family friends who would do anything for her. These are the assets that will help her most in life. Sure, there is statistical evidence that you can get higher-paying jobs with a degree from MIT versus the local community college. But more income doesn't necessarily mean more happiness. Education can't buy us loving spouses and joyful lives. How can I know all this and still be so anxious?

IT IS LATE ON SUNDAY night, and Gabrielle is overwhelmed. She asks me to sit on her bed with her. All weekend, she gave herself to everyone else's demands: a friend with a personal crisis, a boyfriend who wanted to go out, a family that needed a last-minute babysitter. Now she is angry, tearful, behind at school before the week has even started. "And this whole college application thing is feeling like way too much pressure." I want to fix it for her, give her advice on how to make it all better. But instead I ask questions: How can you stay in touch with your own needs? How can you make yourself the priority?

An hour later, I go to bed worried that we'll never find the right college for her. I don't want her to enter into a pressure cooker. But I do want her to get into a school that will help her stretch and grow.

I fall asleep wondering, *Will we ever find a place that will hold her and love her as well as I do?*

NOVEMBER

I am a writer by profession and make a living editing and teaching others to write. Do you think my daughter would let me have just one quick look at her personal essay? No.

We strike a deal. Here is what I cannot do to help: I cannot look at her essay, or look at her applications, or look up deadlines for when her applications are due, or ask her any questions about how it is going.

Here is what I can do to help: address envelopes.

One stack goes to the high school for sending out her transcripts. One stack goes to the teachers she's asking for recommendations. I ask her where the envelopes are that she'll use for the applications. "No one does it that way anymore," she says. "It's all done online these days."

. . . .

Tonight Gabrielle goes online to submit her application to UCLA. It's due December 1, tomorrow. But apparently, every student has waited until Thanksgiving weekend to work on his or her application and is now trying to send it through the Internet on Sunday night. The system is jammed, and she can't send the application she has worked so hard on. "Oh, well. I didn't care that much about UCLA anyway," she says, switching off the computer and heading upstairs to bed.

Her first application deadline. Come and missed. I am left standing in the kitchen, jaw slack, dish towel dangling limp at my side.

DECEMBER

Gabrielle comes to me and says, "I want to be an artist—a real artist—not a commercial artist. That's my gift, I'm sure of it." Her hair is in French braids. She is wearing her high school sweatshirt and sipping chamomile tea. She tells me she can't imagine a life where she isn't doing art every day. Then she asks if I have ever heard of a school that lets the students decide what they want to learn about and provides the resources to go as deep and as long as the student wants.

The only school I know of that lets students do this is her preschool.

Maybe college isn't even the right track for her. We just assume that the smart, enthusiastic, and, yes, privileged high school seniors will head straight to college. But my daughter seems more drawn to "life education" these days. She tells me that she learned more confidence and useful skills at the wilderness horseback riding camp where she works in the summer than she has from all her high school classes this year.

SHE HAS DECIDED that her senior art project will be on homeless people.

JANUARY

As she is going out the door to school, my daughter tells me that she had a dream about skating on thin ice. In the dream, a girl fell through the cracks in front of her and pulled down my daughter's coat and cell phone with her. My daughter couldn't save her.

"Hey, by the way, have you seen that application to NYU?" she asks, a cell phone in one hand, a travel mug of hot chai in the other hand, and a piece of buttered toast dangling from her mouth. "Oh, never mind," she says through the toast, pulling the application out of her messenger bag.

"Don't get chai or toast butter on it," I shout after her. She rolls her eyes and pulls the door closed behind her with her foot.

I KNOW THE JANUARY 15 deadlines are coming up—but I am keeping with my agreement and not mentioning it.

IT'S 9:30 PM on January 14, and Gabrielle comes to me as I'm closing out the kitchen for the night. "I need your help," she says. "Will you look at my essay?"

Here's the trap. At this hour, a rewrite is out of the question. A revision isn't even possible. What could possibly come of my looking at her essay the night before it has to be sent? I could lovingly offer her a wonderful life lesson about taking responsibility for her own procrastination and simply say, "I'm sorry, but I'm too tired." And then go off to bed, leaving her standing slack-jawed in the kitchen. Or I could read her essay, hope it's fine, and if it isn't, push up my sleeves and spend the next three hours helping her make it right. Is this a situation where I can let her fail? Or do I rescue her?

I look at her closely. She has a smattering of stress pimples on her forehead. "Please," she asks, her postbraces retainer making her lisp so that it comes out "Pleathe." I push up my sleeves and follow her to the computer.

ESSAY DONE. I helped her with it only a little. Okay, more than a little. It took about three hours, but it's a winner. I hope we get in.

IT IS NOW 5:40 PM on the evening of January 15, and I am relieved and thrilled that the first round of applications are done, presumably sent into cyberspace hours ago. All we have left are two applications to art colleges, not due until mid-February.

I am making one of Gabrielle's favorite dinners—a curry dish from *The Vegetarian Epicure*—just to celebrate this great accomplishment. One half teaspoon cumin. One teaspoon turmeric. One half teaspoon cayenne. My daughter enters the room.

"I need some help finishing my applications."

"What? You're not done?" I accidentally drop a whole tablespoon of cayenne into the pot. I scrape the red clump of cayenne out of the orange mush of spices. "Why didn't you send it online?"

Gabrielle informs me that she sent her general applications online, but one school wants a graded essay that has to be mailed separately. Something my daughter failed to check until this morning. She doesn't seem aware that this is my "I told you so" moment. I continue to stir.

"Here are my options," she continues. "A short essay about *The Canterbury Tales* or a five-page essay about *Beowulf.*"

I look at the clock. It's 5:45. I'm pretty sure the post office closes at 6:00. It has to be postmarked today. "Let me see them," I suggest, reaching for my reading glasses. I give them both a cursory scan. "Go with the *Beowulf,*" I say.

"Could you at least read them?" she pleads.

I have a string of measuring spoons in my fist, and my fingers are stained with spices. The buttery curry paste in the pot needs stirring or it's going to burn. "Read them? Now?" I ask. I want to shout, "THIS IS IT! THERE IS NO MORE FRICKIN' TIME."

I tersely explain the post office issue: "You can't just drop it in the nearest mailbox and have it postmarked for today." Believe me, I've been there. I know all about manuscripts that have to be postmarked that day. I've ridden this edge, before faxes and emails. "You have to choose an essay now. Use your own judgment. Then get in the car and drive to the post office."

"All right, it's *Beowulf,*" she says, folding it into the envelope. "But can you drive me to the nearest post office? I don't know how to get there."

How will this girl ever survive on her own? I turn off the stove. Driving downtown toward the post office, I do what any self-respecting parent would do in this moment. I shame her. "This is really annoying. You should have taken care of all this earlier."

She swivels her entire body toward me, voice escalating. "When exactly would I have had time to do this today? I was at school until four, and then I had a piano lesson."

"I mean earlier, as in two months ago."

She looks out the window. It's 5:55 PM. And dark and raining.

We pull into the post office at 5:58. The sign says it closes at 6:30. We're half an hour early.

"See. We had plenty of time," she tells me, huffing out of the car.

GABRIELLE INVITES ME to look at one of the art school catalogs with her tonight. As we're flipping through the pages, she suddenly gets teary. "I can't do this," she says. "I don't want to leave my friends, or my school, or even my family. This whole college pressure is horrible. I hate how it forces you to leave the life you love."

WE ASK GABRIELLE to pick up her clutter around the house before she heads out tonight. "I am so ready to move out of here," she mutters, gathering up her five coats, four purses, and nine pairs of shoes.

FEBRUARY

Gabrielle has worked all month on getting her art materials sent out to the two art schools she is applying to. The dining room table has been turned into her studio—chalk, acrylics, charcoal sketches splayed everywhere. I have been impressed with her diligence.

It feels like she has figured out what she cares about and has been willing to commit herself to it.

Now it is the day that all her materials must be sent by overnight mail. "Mama," she calls out as I walk past the dining room. "Could you please help me with my application?"

"I thought this was all you had to do. There's an application, too?" Body getting hot. Heart pumping.

"I know. It's just way too much," she says, as if we're complaining about the art school's demands and not her complete disorganization. "But it's only a formality—they mostly care about the art. Anyway, I'm a little behind, and I was wondering if you could just type in the answers to some of the questions that I haven't finished yet while I finish this watercolor." She swishes her brush in a glass of murky water.

I pull up the "routine" application on the computer, expecting a name, address, and extracurricular activities kind of application. I discover questions such as "Do you think it's important that artists speak or write about their work?" and "Describe an event or idea that has been very important to you." Most of them are answered, as she promised, but there are a few that are blank.

As I start to scroll through the application, there's a knock at the door. The cable guy is here. I forgot. Today is the day I scheduled to have my Internet cable installed. It took me weeks to get this appointment. I lead him into my office. "Can you turn off the computer for a while?" he asks, holding up a drill.

It is after 3:00. The entire package has to be at the UPS store by 4:00. "No," I say. "We're working on a college application."

"We?" he asks, raising an eyebrow.

I resist the urge to explain myself, explain the whole mess of pro-crastination and ambivalence that's plagued our house since September. "Yep. Down to the wire here. So can I keep it on while you work?" I turn my face to the screen and call out to my daughter. "Okay, we're going to have to talk over the drilling."

Somehow we get it done. My daughter and I grab her artwork. I print out her application, and we jump in the car. As I speed toward the UPS store, she sprays hairspray on all her chalk draw-ings. We arrive with nine minutes to spare.

ON THE WAY HOME, I turn to her at a stoplight and lay my hand atop hers. "Why has this been so hard to do ahead of time?" I ask.

Gabrielle is silent for a moment. "Maybe the reason I waited so long is that I'm afraid I won't get in anywhere." The Seattle winter sun is low in the sky, giving her face a golden-pink sheen. "Maybe it would feel really horrible to try my very hard-est and be rejected. If I slap it all together at the last minute and I don't get in anywhere, at least I could tell myself that I didn't really try that hard."

MARCH

This is the waiting month. There is nothing I can say or do to help, but I try anyway.

"The truth is, I really believe you will get accepted somewhere," I tell Gabrielle as she eats Heath Bar Crunch ice cream straight from the carton. "But if you don't, we'll just start looking into other options. I know you'll find your way."

She smiles weakly and continues scooping. Six rejections. Could one high school girl hold that much disappointment?

APRIL

The six results are in. Two rejections—one from her "safety" and one from her "reach" school. Two waitlists—both from schools she liked. Two acceptances—one from the school she liked the least and one from the art school that she most wanted to get into. It's a good list—some disappointments, but much elation, too. We open a bottle of champagne, toast her, and call the grandparents.

"She got into her first-choice school," I tell my mother on the phone, watching Gabrielle twirl around the kitchen with her father. I mentally note that I have used the word "she" instead of "we." The cable guy was right. Hard as I've tried this year, I haven't been successful at extracting myself from the process.

Maybe now, I can finally let go.

MAY

Tonight, Gabrielle presents her senior art project at the high school. As it turns out, she did indeed make portraits of homeless people, some of whom she met while handing out sandwiches to men and women living on the streets. But she also made portraits of people from other walks of life—strangers on city buses, her close friends, her younger brother, even us, her parents. She tells the audience that each portrait, like each person, had a life of its own. As a creator, it was sometimes challenging to let the art be what it wanted to be.

I think back to when she was in preschool so many years ago—

the one that let her go as long and as deep as she yearned to. Gabrielle spent her time drawing portraits of unicorn ponies surrounded by swirly purple flowers and fat yellow suns. Her resources were as follows: a box of markers, an endless supply of scrap paper, and permission to do what she loved.

Seeing her now, with her collection of painted canvases, I realize it doesn't really matter where she goes to college. Yes, this Buddha moment is partially sponsored by the fact that she got into a school of her choice. But for tonight, I know with certainty that she is on a path that will take her as far and deep as she wants to go. As for the resources? Just look at her. She already possesses everything she needs to find her way.

POSTSCRIPT

Over the summer, Gabrielle decides to defer college for a year. She's clear that it's the right choice for a number of reasons: the obvious ambivalence she's felt all along, her desire to travel and get a nonclassroom education for a while. Her school has allowed her to postpone her enrollment to the following fall. She has saved up enough money to travel through the South Pacific with a friend for six months.

It is now late November, one week before her departure. Gabrielle comes to me, a mug of green tea between the palms of her hands, as if in prayer.

"I've been thinking. I'm not sure that art school is going to be enough for me. I also want to learn more about international politics. So I'd like to apply to a few more schools before I leave. Do you think I have time to pull together a new essay before I go?"

Tell
It
Like
It Is

The Color of T-shirts

Elizabeth Nunez

I GREW UP IN a middle-class Victorian home in Trinidad, a former colony of England. It may seem strange to some that I describe my home as Victorian, for if you see me, you will know that included in my ancestry are bloodlines that go back to Africa. But the point of colonization was to create subjects for the mother country, and we in the middle class did our best to imitate English manners and English culture. I learned to keep a stiff upper lip in hard times, to hold my emotions in check in good times, and, above all, to restrain myself from overt expressions of affection in public. I knew my parents loved me, but there was little hugging and kissing in our home. I was determined, though, that when I had a child of my own, I would change that.

I had been living in New York for some years when John, my son, was born. With no family members or friends from back home to keep me in check, I lavished affection on him. In photo album after photo album, there are pictures of the two of us, glued together: He is kissing me, I am kissing him. He has his arms around me, mine are around him, and I am smiling at him as if nothing and no one in the world could make me happier.

John, I used to say, loved loving. He was not self-conscious about hugging me in front of his friends or telling me that he loved me. When he was in grade school, we used to wait for his school bus together, standing behind the glass sliding door of the kitchen even though it exposed us fully to the street corner where his school-mates gathered. John would hug me tightly around my neck and kiss me as soon as the bus was in sight, and then turn back several times as he crossed the street to shout, "Bye, Mom! Love you, Mom." Then one day, when he was in fourth grade, he tugged me away from the glass door. "Not here, Mom," he pleaded with me as I tried to plant a big kiss on his cheek. "Here." He led me to a spot behind the kitchen wall. The next day, in his eagerness to avoid me, he ran out of the kitchen to the bus, leaving his lunch box behind. I ran after him. "John, John!" I shouted. "Your lunch box!" He ran faster. It didn't take much for me to realize that my son was not merely running toward the bus; *he was running away from me.*

My first reaction was to assume I had embarrassed him, for let me confess that I am not the prettiest sight in the morning. My hair is usually uncombed, my nightie hanging below an old terry cloth robe that should have been discarded years ago, mismatched socks rolled over my ankles. I suppose I didn't want to face the fact that my relationship with my son was changing. It was easier to con-vince myself that all I needed to do was to improve my morning wardrobe. But in spite of my efforts to look as close as I could at breakfast to a version of the wife on *Ozzie and Harriet*, John persisted in disowning me in the presence of his friends. He would give me a quick kiss behind the wall and sprint to the bus, not once turning back to say goodbye. He was growing up; he was leaving his boyhood days. A preteen, he had an instinctive need to carve out space between him and me. It was a need that shattered my comfortable world but one that also turned out to be dangerous for him. My son, you see, is an African American male, and in this country where I had chosen to raise him, African American males often find themselves suspect.

I SHOULD HAVE BEEN prepared for the dangers my son would confront when he declared his independence from me. In the Brooklyn hospital where he was born, I had more than a warning of what was to come. The evening before I was to be discharged, I packed my suitcase, barely able to contain my excitement that finally, at last, I would have my baby to myself without nurses dictating when and where. A young intern abruptly entered my room, his eyes downcast on the clipboard in his hands, his pen poised businesslike to write. I could not take my son home with me the next day, he informed me. "We've made our report to the Department of Social Services. A social worker will be here soon to explain."

Of course, the first thought that came to my mind was that something had happened to my son. "What? What?" The muscles in my throat were so constricted, I could barely get the words out. "You should know," the intern responded. "You are responsible."

Responsible? Responsible for what? The social worker who

came minutes later clarified *what* for me. "For the heroin you transferred to your son," she said. "We are treating him now, but we have
reported you as an abusive mother. You can't take him home."

What followed next is still a blur in my mind. I remember pushing up the sleeves of my robe and extending my arm toward her. I
remember the stream of words that fell out of my mouth, a crazy
woman babbling. "Where? Where?" I was shouting. The social
worker came closer and looked at my bared arm. Nothing. No tell-
tale needle marks. She saw her mistake, but there were no apologies.

Because my son had been restless that night, tossing and turning
in his bed, crying incessantly, vomiting his milk—*because my son is
black*—the attending doctor assumed. And what he assumed was
that my son was experiencing withdrawal from an addictive drug,
which his mother, *because she was black*, had passed on to him.

The next day, Saturday, I was not allowed to bring my son home.
The hospital gave me a bogus excuse about needing to observe
John for one more day. I know now that they were unable to release
him to me without the permission of the Department of Social
Services, which did not open until Monday.

So, yes, I was heartbroken, but also scared, when my son decided
it was time to break away from me. I knew black teenage boys still
needed plenty of protection. Henry, my ex-husband's son from his
first marriage, needed my protection, though he, too, like John,
thought otherwise.

When Henry was fourteen, his sole goal, it seemed, was to oppose
whatever his father told him to do. At first blush, his behavior

appeared to be no more than normal teenage rebellion: the boy in a battle with his father to claim his manhood. As I reflect on those days now, I can see more clearly that behind his bravado was a deep-seated fear that he had lost his father to me and his younger brother. So much of what we learn as parents is in hindsight, long after the children are grown. Perhaps that is why grandparents are so solicitous—sometimes, in the opinion of many parents, overbearing. They know the mistakes they have made. I should have done more to reassure Henry that he was as loved as his brother, that as much as his brother, he was part of the family.

Henry was not allowed to ride his motor scooter without his father's permission, but that stricture seemed only to guarantee that he would do the opposite. One day, he came home from the prep school he attended, and still in his school uniform of navy blue blazer, tie, and gray pants, he jumped on his scooter, with his school friend clasping his waist from behind.

I got the call late in the evening from the police, informing me that Henry was in their custody. The detective who met me at the precinct told me that Henry would have been a taillight on his bumper if he had not stopped his scooter when he did. *A taillight!* The detective's tone implied that I should be grateful he had spared Henry's life. Henry's version of what happened was that just as he was dropping off his friend at his street corner, he saw the police car, and aware that he had disobeyed his father, and, additionally, that he was not wearing a helmet, he tried to outrace the car. The detective's version was that Henry had dropped off a mule and was trying to escape.

A mule?

The detective explained: the guy who carries the drugs.

What led the police to conclude that two boys in prep school uniforms, one with his book bag on his back, were dealers on their way to drop off drugs? I could reach only one conclusion: They fit a racial profile entrenched in the minds of too many people. I was angry, but I felt helpless. Henry begged me not to file a complaint. He feared retribution from the officers who stopped him. I swore to myself then that John would never find himself in a similar situation.

BUT WHEN JOHN turned fourteen, he too wanted his independence from his father and me. One day, he decided that he would find his own way with his friends to a football match in the next town, some miles from our suburban neighborhood. It was late autumn, and by the time he was ready to leave home, it had already turned dark. After much wrangling, I managed to negotiate a compromise. I would drive him and his three friends to the game but leave them on the corner, four blocks away from the football field, just in case, heaven forbid, some of his classmates would see him with his mother. Anxiety gripping my heart, I made him promise to call me when the game was over.

I must have been back home just fifteen minutes when the phone rang. It was John, thank God, not the police, but it was because of the police he called. Two officers had stopped him and his friends. They wanted to know where they were going. They were black boys in a white neighborhood. What were they doing there at that hour of the evening? I had already taught my son how to respond to the police. Say "Yes, sir. No, sir," I had told him. They have the power. But John was a teenager feeling his oats. Why, he wanted to know from the police, had they stopped them? When the police had no answer for him, he demanded their names and badge numbers.

John never gave me more details than these. He and his friends were in a sour mood when I picked them up. What should have been a pleasurable memory of their teenage years was now a painful one. They had lost interest in the game. All the excitement that less than an hour ago had them slapping each other high fives and laughing uproariously at a joke, which, of course, was funnier because it was incomprehensible to me, was now sucked out of them like wind from a balloon. Their still-childish faces were creased with frowns, their lips puckered into pouts. I watched sadly as they adopted a posture of machismo in a vain attempt to block out the humiliation they had endured.

There were other incidents during John's teenage years when his determination to stand on his own two feet, to become a man, proved costly to him simply because he is black. I often wondered about the effect such experiences had on his psyche. He was an adult, twenty-six, already earning his living in the corporate world, when I asked him. He reminded me of the time he played soccer in the third grade. Though we lived in a black neighborhood, we were zoned into a white school district. (It is no secret that Long Island is one of the most segregated communities on the northeast coast.) John was often the only black child in his class, or maybe one of two. On the soccer field, he was usually the only black player. I found the games excruciating to witness, especially when his team played another Long Island (and all-white) team. What was going through his mind as he fought for the home team and against the visiting team? Did he feel different, alone, isolated? "Oh, none of that, Mom," he had reassured me, a nine-year-old already wise beyond his years. "I see blue T-shirts, and I see red T-shirts," he said, as if oblivious to skin color. "I know I have to beat the red T-shirts."

John tells me now that he never sensed my anxiety when I questioned him then about his feelings about the soccer teams. I suppose I did what most parents do: I put on a face for my child, a buffer to protect him from the fears that seized my heart. We parents know that too soon, experience will teach our children that the world is not always kind, so we do what we can to prolong their days of innocence.

John tells me something else, too, that catches me by surprise. It is from me, he says, that he learned not to allow racism to intimidate him into forgoing his ambitions. And I realize that the Victorian, black middle-class home in Trinidad where I was raised prepared me more than I thought to be a mother of a black male child in America. With their lessons about keeping a stiff upper lip, about guarding my emotions, my parents taught me to be strong in times of adversity, to be self-reliant, to close my ears to my detractors, to listen to my own heart, to work hard, to remain focused. They believed that if I did these things, no obstacles would be insurmountable.

Sofie's Boots

Susan Hodara

THESE DAYS, SHE seems to lack the conviction to push the words from her throat, so they slide out through nearly unmoving lips in a monotone that can barely be heard. Her ice-blue eyes slip from sparkling to expressionless, from deeply empathetic to cold and cruel. Dressed most often in paint-spattered clothing, her jeans slung low on her narrow hips, my teenage daughter, Sofie, seesaws between the exuberance of her younger years, the zest with which she once embraced the moments of her days, and a more recent, more dominant mix of defiance, cynicism, and exhaustion.

She is still beautiful, her skin pale, peachy, and lightly freckled, her face open and wise beneath her golden-brown hair. But adolescence has lodged itself within her, throwing her off balance, leaving her aloof and often sad. To her, I have lately become inadequate, clueless, or simply annoying. She is barely seventeen, drowning in demands from school, friends, and too much to do in too little time, drained by the taste of disappointment seeping into her days. She has the world ahead of her, but she rarely believes it anymore.

Which is meant to explain why I spent nearly $300 on her birthday present, why I abandoned my plans and rearranged my Sunday morning when she bounded cheerily into my bedroom and said: "Mom, get ready! Let's go get the boots!"

Sofie had spotted the boots in a small shop on the Upper West Side months earlier on a day we had no time to try them on, let alone check the price. She tugged at my sleeve, and though she saw them for probably only several seconds, they took up residence in her consciousness, an objectification of a part of herself that she seemed to need to claim.

They are flat-soled and knee-high, made of soft, tan suede. Their style might best be described as urban Native American, with fringe around the top edges, a few small beaded patterns of red, black, and white, and a feather dangling from the back of each. A leather lace crisscrosses up the calf and ties at the top. When we returned to the store that afternoon, they sat where we'd first seen them in the window, flopped in unison to one side.

"This is our last pair," the salesgirl told us. She was young, lanky, and chic.

"Size 7," the other girl informed us. This one was shorter and plump and also chic. The boots fit Sofie perfectly, hugging her slender calves as if happy to be home. She clutched herself, twisting side to side before the mirror and beaming.

"Then it was meant to be," we all agreed, the girls nodding and assuring Sofie that the boots were "her," and by the time we asked

the price, we'd practically already bought them. There was a giddi-
ness in the store, empty but for us, and the tall girl told the short
one, "I remember when my mother used to buy me things I loved."

The choice between guilt at the extravagance and the wish to
recognize the resurfacing of Sofie's recently absent enthusiasm was
an easy one, and I was comforted by the buoyancy of her spirit on
our drive home from the city, her still-booted legs bent at the knees,
her feet propped against the glove compartment to allow full view
of her new acquisition.

The fact that Sofie has not worn the boots since, that they sit on
display in the corner of her bedroom, one slumped over against the
soft, suede body of the other, does not negate the brief interlude of
happiness that soon faded against the reappearance of flatness and
irritation. It does, though, remind me of many things I already knew
but chose to forget: that the joy of new clothing is as short-lived as
its fabric is thin; and that the difference between who we want to
be and who we have the courage to be is sometimes insurmountable, at least for a time.

Occasionally now I suggest, in a casual tone that I hope conveys
insouciance, "How about the boots? They'd look great with what
you're wearing!" Sofie doesn't respond. Her mouth is set, her eyes
withdraw into a gauzy distance; I am silently dismissed as she pushes
past me toward the hall. When she leaves for school, I stand for a
moment in her doorway to look at the boots that have come to
seem forlorn, and to remember that even a mother's love is often
unable to make things right for a teenager.

Runaway

Debra Gwartney

IN THE SPRING OF 1997, I drove across the state of Oregon, from ocean to desert, twice a month. Every other Friday after work, I gathered my two youngest daughters, along with baggies of crayons and stacks of paper for drawing; a shoebox of Disney soundtracks, *The Little Mermaid, Aladdin, Mary Poppins,* for singing along to; four juice boxes, a package of string cheese, apples, and foil-wrapped chocolate chip cookies for the sister at the end of our trip, and we'd head out of town on the cool McKenzie River Highway. On to the shadowed Santiam Pass. Past Hoodoo, through Sisters: enter Bend. It was the last curve of the road before the relentless strip of asphalt that split Eastern Oregon all the way to Burns.

Burns. That's where Amanda was staying with a bony rancher, his arthritic wife, and their two cowboy-hatted, tight-jeaned boys. That's where I'd go to find my sixteen-year-old daughter, who'd been given a title I could not bring myself to say aloud: foster child.

. . . .

THE 180-MILE STRETCH of State Highway 20 between Bend and Burns is not a ribbon. It's a straight black line with no end in sight in either direction—you lose track of the place you've been two minutes after you leave it. Not until you're on its borders do you see the place you're going. In between, the dark road cuts the land in half, a mark in the sand with a bully on either side, blown-out acres of sagebrush and tumbling tumbleweed. Distant mountains get farther away instead of closer, or seem to, as you travel the steady miles: The land is that flat. Telephone poles and barbed wire fences, upon which are perched crows, red-tailed hawks, and an occasional red-winged blackbird, are the land's only ornamentation; the fence line wobbles and weaves in the side window of the moving car. For three hours, the slanted sun has nothing to pierce but your eyes.

On one of those drives—this one in early April—I passed the shut-down gas station at Brothers and glanced in the rearview mirror to see that the girls had fallen asleep, one on top of the other; Mollie's head on Mary's leg and Mary leaning against the window with a feather pillow between her cheek and the glass. Their plastic families of elephants, wolves, and polar bears—mothers and babies—were tumbled across the seat. This set of daughters, eleven and nine, was smart enough to know the best way to get through the tedious part of the drive. Otherwise, it was impossible to keep the monotony from digging into the knobbed bone at the base of your neck, where it would stay the whole trip. I turned down my music—on this tape, twenty-one Van Morrison songs that equaled seventy-four miles—so as not to wake them.

We'd ordered drive-thru on our way through Bend and ate as we left town. Pale buns and gray meat, ketchup that smelled sticky, and smoky, grease-crisped French fries. We didn't eat this way at home. But somehow it felt like a fitting experience between our house and theirs—plus, it was a quick stop, only a minor delay in getting to Amanda.

Now the remnants of the meal, wadded wrappers and flattened condiment packets, were stuffed in a sack that sat on the passenger seat along with the box of food I'd brought from home and a plastic container in case Mary had to throw up, a common occurrence on our trips. The smell of grease and damp paper hovered near the ceiling of the car; the steering wheel was coated with oil that had stayed on my skin after eating.

I reached into my purse for a tube of ChapStick, mint-clean enough to dissipate the scent of dinner, and my fingers hit the hard plastic edges of a CD stored in my bag. Two CDs, actually, rock/punk bands the names of which Amanda had once mentioned and that had for some reason stuck with me. The day before we'd left on this trip, I'd gone to the music store near our house and spent money I didn't have on the albums. Then I dropped by the bookstore for a used Steinbeck novel and a collection of Adrienne Rich poetry, knowing each item would be more troubling than the last to the Ranchers. They'd call the organization that had arranged the living situation to complain that I had, once again, delivered contraband. "This'll never work," I could hear Donna saying, "unless our rules are respected." The head guy would tell me to stop bringing such gifts, but I wouldn't. I was only going to be ordered around so much concerning my own child. The bimonthly visits, for instance. Donna had made it clear that she preferred I stayed away, let her work on my daughter for a half a year or more and straighten out the parts she considered kinked before she sent her back to me.

The rancher woman would find it strange, I suspected, that I'd not been willing to buy this kind of music—which I was now toting these miles for Amanda—for my kids in the past. I tolerated the albums when they came in, but I didn't particularly want the Ramones or the Subhumans or even young, woeful, dead Kurt Cobain in the house. Novels and poetry, yes. Anything they wanted to read, except for Burroughs' book *Junky,* which I tore in half and threw away when I found it on Stephanie's bed. I hadn't banished their music, but I hadn't been keen on it.

I'd never believed in trying to be my daughters' friend. Other parents set out from day one, it seemed to me, to be pals with their kids, confidants and coconspirators. With none of my girls did I whisper about boys or giggle over clothes. They went upstairs to do that with each other; I stayed down to cook and do laundry and look over the half-done homework they'd stranded on the kitchen table. But now, with my second daughter, Stephanie, off in Montana with friends, separated from us for at least six months, and Amanda living with strangers who subscribed to *Range* magazine and decorated their living room with elk antlers and Hummel statues, I didn't mind being thought of as a friend. At least as a friendly presence. Someone who showed up with Amanda's brand of music, with her taste in films and art, and even with a few fashion magazines—which I wouldn't have allowed back home, all that cleavage and hair and perfume samples I'd smell for weeks—that she could hide under her bed out of Donna's sight.

Amanda looked forward to my every-other-weekend visits as if they alone were keeping her alive. I became attached to them in the same way, not ready yet—especially while driving the last miles to her temporary house where I'd be embraced with a fervor I hadn't felt for years—to realize how she'd someday seethe. After all, I was the one who'd agreed to this "placement." It was only a matter of time, of weeks, maybe, until she'd despise me for the distance I had put between her and Stephanie, for these months they could not speak on the telephone, their letters to one another read first by therapists who searched for secret messages and private codes. But I hadn't been implicated for that—not yet, anyway. Each time I wound up the hill to the Ranchers' house and crunched across the gravel driveway, I arrived as a distraction and a delight. Her rescuer.

THE REASONS FOR the foster home were fairly straightforward: Amanda and Stephanie had hit the streets in early January. After they'd been gone for more than a week, I hired a man to go find them, and he did. This man, an ex–L.A. cop and Runaway Seeker with a huge neck and meaty hands, transported them to the offices of a wilderness therapy outfit I'd heard about from our family therapist. One cold Sunday, I met my oldest daughters, so pissed at their plucking that they wouldn't talk to or touch me, at the Albany headquarters; an hour later, I stood on the sidewalk with my coat wrapped around me tight against the sleet and my hat pulled down to my eyes as Amanda left with one group and Stephanie with another.

Each girl was stuffed in a forest green van and sent off to the dead-of-winter Cascade Mountains. I was told there would be ten, eleven, twelve feet of snow to hike through and camp in each night for three weeks. "Nature is the best teacher," I heard from the psychologist who ran the program. "Nature is the best counselor." Twenty-one days of lentils and beans they'd cook themselves on a fire they'd start themselves with wet wood and without matches (instead: flint and steel). No shower, no laundry, no bed to sleep on. No drugs, no beer, no cigarettes, or boys to sleep with. "Let nature do its work and issue its consequences," he told the solemn, pasty-faced group of parents as we clutched paper coffee cups and stared into the brown liquid like the answers to our troubles might rise out of the steam.

I sent my daughters on the wilderness trip as a last resort—at least, what felt like a last resort then—borrowing from my father half of the thousands of dollars it took to pay for the "life-cleansing excursions," as the brochure promised, and squeezing my ex-husband for the other half. I sent them believing that three weeks would cure us all and we'd start over.

But instead of spending the twenty-one days of the trek figuring out the future like I was supposed to, planning how to "re-parent" my daughters, as the psychologist had suggested at the family meeting, I sat around in the evenings after work and during the weekends waiting for news that Amanda and Steph were okay, that they were "opening up," "coming clean," "facing their issues." These were the phrases I heard from one or another young counselor who'd hiked to the nearest telephone for my once-a-week check-in. At the conclusion of the allotted fifteen minutes, I was often more confused than when the call began. What was going on really? Were they cold? Hungry? Did they miss me? And what was going to be different, in them and in me, when this was done?

"Oh, yes, sure, she's homesick. She talks about you. She wants to come home," the counselors told me. And yet, none of them gave me a clue as to how to make that work.

Then the weather got bad enough that the head psychologist radioed the separate groups and told them to gather at the warmth and safety of the main wall tent, a large canvas room set up in a mountain meadow. As they neared the tent, Stephanie said the counselors refused to acknowledge what she knew in her gut: that Amanda was nearby. She'd be somehow silenced if she called her sister's name, so instead she began to sing—Blondie songs, ones she and Amanda had long before, at twelve or thirteen, learned by heart and recited with Deborah Harry's exact squeaky intonation.

Stephanie belted out the music, and Amanda, on her side of the woods, heard. Finally, even the head counselor knew he couldn't stop them from finding each other, so he cut a deal. A half hour together, and don't ask again. The girls agreed. What did they talk about? They didn't remember exactly, except that Stephanie took Amanda's fingers in one palm and asked her big sister, "How did you keep your fingernail polish from chipping off in the cold?" Then they were pulled apart again; they didn't see each other again for six months.

. . . .

AT THE MEETING at the end of the three weeks, the psychologist and his team of young flannel-shirted counselors announced they didn't think Amanda and Stephanie should return home yet. It would take a minimum of six months to cure them of the street— to rid them of the high that came from sleeping in abandoned buildings and spare-changing on street corners, drifting off at night on a wave of 40s or pot or some new drug I'd never heard of—to get them to let go of each other. I accepted the advice with a raw relief. Until the counselors told me my daughters shouldn't come back, I hadn't known how terrified I'd been about their return. Best of all, I could blame the decision on the experts.

Friends in the deep woods of Montana, seventy miles from any town and five hundred miles from me, volunteered to take fourteen-year-old Stephanie, but Amanda would go to strangers. Who else could keep her from running? I couldn't think of anyone, family or friends. The trek leader knew the Burns folks, fourth generation on their ranch, who needed help cooking for the hired hands at harvest and extra daily support for Donna, whose fingers curled into claws and whose knobbed knees wouldn't let her stand quite straight. Their house sat at the top of a sheer cliff, the face of which was as wide and pale as a drive-in movie screen. To get to the highway on foot from there was nearly impossible, and no cars or trucks passing by would pick up this waif of a girl, so obviously out of place.

DONNA AND BILL were long ago in their beds (up before dawn) when I finally drove the car across the dark parking area behind the house. A shadow flitted along beside us: Amanda. She'd been wait-

ing under the eaves even though it was a chilly night, clear and biting. I slowed down so she could open the passenger door and slip
into the seat. Without a word she breathed deep and reached over
to take my hand.

"You're freezing," I said, and she pressed my fingers together. I
pulled in at the guest cottage, a remodeled outbuilding at the edge
of the pasture that Donna called her "bed-and-breakfast nook," for
which she charged me $65 a night but most of the time rented (for
a better price, I imagined) to the just-married and just-graduated
from Burns High School, young couples who didn't have the
money to even get over to Bend for a night's honeymoon and
couldn't leave the chores on the ranch for more than a few hours
anyway. The following day, the newlyweds would join Donna and
Bill and the boys for bacon and eggs and French toast with whipped
cream and oversweetened frozen strawberries before getting back to
their own place and a lifetime of togetherness.

Under the twinkling stars, Amanda helped me unload the bags
from the back of the car, carrying them through the open door of
the cottage as quietly as we could: Neither of us wanted Donna to
appear on the porch to see what the fuss was about. We got Mary
and Mollie roused enough to roll them one at a time onto the
unfolded sofa bed, a bear baby still tucked in Mollie's hand. When
we were settled, I dead-bolted the door from the inside. For this
night, the Ranchers would have nothing to do with us.

I changed into my nightgown and got into my bed. Amanda
stretched out next to me on top of the covers, still dressed but shoe-
less, and began to speak to me of things she wouldn't have if we'd

been home, if Stephanie had been anywhere near and they could slip off together. She told me about a teacher who'd complimented her essay on *A Separate Peace* and who'd said there wasn't another student at Burns High who could read at that depth. She told me about some boys who'd caught her outside one day during lunch and doused her with a bucket of muddy water and called her a slut because her hair was dyed black, instead of the streaked blond most Burns girls sported, and because her tongue was pierced, which they were sure had something to do with oral sex. She described the way Donna and Bill's sons ignored her most of the time and got their dad to give her the worst jobs—shoveling cow shit or cleaning the stifling henhouse. The boys had given her a kitten from a feral litter when she first arrived but neglected to tell her not to let it outside: Coyotes got it after a day or two, though Amanda had never stopped looking.

She begged me to take her home. It would be different now, she said. She'd mind my rules. She'd go to school; she wanted to go to school. There'd be no drugs, no running off for days, no wild boys or booze or hair dyeing or cigarettes. No overdoses of Tylenol or threats to do so. No cutting into her arms and legs with everything from a paper clip to a Swiss Army knife. I promise, I promise, she said.

She didn't mention Stephanie, though I suspected she was asking to let them both come home. I didn't say her name either. Stephanie was two states away, inaccessible. And I was right there. We were friends, Amanda and I. It would be too dangerous to alienate each other; after foster care, what was there? That was a void both of us knew to stay back from.

"Mama, please," she said as she pressed herself under my arm, using the name for me that came out only with the most plaintive requests. "Get me out of here."

It didn't matter if I believed her promises to change, the temptation was charged in me—I wanted to head straight into the house the next morning and tell Donna, who'd already be giving me the "Mothers like you don't deserve children" look, that Amanda was packing her bags and we were going, the four of us, back to Eugene. Then I'd whisper in Amanda's ear: *See? We are in this together.* I knew how Donna introduced her to the people at church, and at their weekly 4-H meetings, and at the Sears where she went to buy jeans and shoes and her plain cotton blouses: "This is Amanda. Our foster child." Back home, every time I thought of it I fought the urge to drive to Burns and demand her back.

But I couldn't. I'd made a deal with the psychologist to see it through until July. The desire for the streets and for drugs wouldn't be broken in her otherwise, he was sure of it. The minute she and Stephanie saw each other, they'd be back with their friends, the so-called "mall rats" of our town, or they'd jump on a freight train to somewhere else. Even without Stephanie, after a couple of days, Amanda would be drawn out by her old friends, both the human ones and the substance ones, and I'd be the enemy again. And wasn't that the best reason to keep her in Burns as long as possible? It felt so inside of me: The Ranchers got the sullen Amanda—polite to a fault, not a single rude word or bad attitude, but not alive in the way a girl her age should be—and I got to sweep in once every fourteen days to be cherished. I despised Donna and Bill and their silly sons, as well as every person in this town for what they assumed about Amanda's bad home life, but so what? I'd take it all, I'd swallow Donna's tsk-tsking about my lax and liberal ways, if I got this other part of the deal: Right now, my daughter adored me.

AFTER BREAKFAST IN Donna's kitchen the next morning, a hamburger-egg-cheese casserole and toasted white bread, Amanda wanted to walk me around the ranch. Donna had made her boys promise that they'd give Mary and Mollie a ride in the small wagon, pulled with a four-wheeler they were allowed to drive on ranchland, and then take them to see the recently born kid goats. Once my youngest daughters were nestled in the hay of the wagon and sitting far enough back that they wouldn't bounce out if the boys hit a bump, I went on the tour with Amanda. A breeze blew a fine skiff of dirt around us as we wandered among the outbuildings; tufts of tall grass swayed in the dry pastures. The spring air was warm enough that I took off my sweater and tied it around my waist as we stood against the fence that bordered the couple acres closest to the house. Other fields, alfalfa and hay, were far away, farther than I could see, and from here the hundreds of head of cattle—off now grazing on federal lands—from which Bill and Donna earned their income were only a faint smell.

"I want to show you something," Amanda said, and took my hand. She led me to a small shed where a cow rested in one of the stalls, two small calves bawling at her side. One of the babies was big-eyed with long, black lashes and had a coat of smooth brown with a few white spots. When I got closer to the wood barrier, leaning up against it with Amanda at my side, I was able to see the other calf better in the dim shadows of the shed. This one's coat was ragged, roughed up as if someone had combed it the wrong way. Its eyes were half-closed, weepy; its legs skinnier than the other baby's and not quite straight.

"What's wrong with it?" I asked her.

Amanda told me that the cow had given birth to twins a few days before, but that one of the babies had died soon after birth, still moist from her mother's womb. Amanda had helped Bill wrap the dead one in a tarp and put it out back of the shed. That very afternoon, Bill had found a newborn calf in the field trying to suckle from its dead mother's teat. He'd brought the calf in—it was the one in front of us right now, Amanda said. He'd unwrapped the dead calf from the plastic tarp and skinned it, then he grafted that coat onto this one's body. The decomposing coat hung on the sickly baby like a bad toupee, but Amanda said Bill was going to give it another couple of days.

"He's hoping the calf will smell enough like her baby that the cow will take it on as her own," she said, reaching her hand out to try to coax the calf over for a nuzzle. When he didn't move toward her, she dropped her hand, then turned to me, one of her feet up on the rail in a cowgirl stance I hadn't seen before. "But I don't know," she said. "It doesn't look to me like it's working."

AMANDA AND I LEFT the calves, the sick one and the well one, and headed back to the house. That afternoon we'd go into Burns, and I'd buy her a new pair of tennis shoes and sparkling eye shadow, and during our hour of shopping I'd think about the baby cows, about the difference between being a foster mother and the mother of a foster child—the thorn that was under my skin. And then, driving back, I'd feel a new edge in my daughter. She wasn't going to stay friendly with me much longer; something about the day had made that clear. The end of my tolerance for this situation was forming in me, as well, hard and flat as a river rock, the perfect kind for skipping across the water's surface. We weren't going to make it to July. As soon as I could manage, I had to get Amanda out of there.

By the middle of May, I'd found a Youth Corps in Eugene that wanted to hire her as a summer trail builder. I called Amanda one Monday afternoon, right after school, and told her to get a ride to Bend the next day, whatever she had to do. I'd meet her there. The following Saturday, she'd leave for six weeks of wilderness work—no "opening up" or "coming clean" or "nature as counselor," just ten hours a day of steady, hard work. I didn't speak to Donna or Bill or the wilderness trek psychologist, I just went about the plan. Tuesday afternoon, while Donna was taking the boys to the doctor, Amanda left a brief note on their counter, saying that she'd hitched a ride with one of her teacher's friends who was off to Bend on an errand and that she wouldn't be back. That night, I found her in the parking lot of the Buffalo Drive-Thru, the very place Mary and Mollie and I had ordered meals a month before. Amanda called out, "Shotgun," got in the front seat, and we went home.

SEVEN YEARS HAVE passed since Amanda left Burns, and in that time, Amanda, Stephanie, and I have begun to make peace with each other. They are grown daughters now, with their own lives and aspirations and their own sense of what it means to be a family. There's little anger among us, although the residue of those long years of difficulty sticks to us no matter what we do to wash it away. Part of the reason it's still around, I believe, is because things got worse before they got better, and I had to face the truth that there was nothing I could do to keep my daughters from leaving me. Amanda came home from Burns, Stephanie from Montana, and before I could even imagine such a possibility, they were gone again. This second time they went far away, farther than any ex–L.A. cop could look. The wilderness trek sheded from them like so much bad skin, the long separation from each other and from their sisters and me a futile exercise. The months at the ranch forgotten. Near Christmas 1997, days after her seventeenth birthday, Amanda would get arrested in Tucson and I'd fly her home to enter a drug clinic. Stephanie would disappear for a year.

Did I ruin our chance of reconciliation by pulling Amanda out of Burns too early? I used to think so, but I don't anymore. It wouldn't have mattered how long she or Stephanie had stayed under someone else's watch. In the end, they had to go and keep going until they decided to return. I must have known that on some level, hard as it was to accept. When they left the second time, I didn't try to stop them.

I REMEMBER THE EXACT day: Amanda freshly home from her second stint with the Youth Corps, which has left her burly strong and well-funded, $1,500 stashed away in the bank. Stephanie, returned from Montana, defiant and egging Amanda for a new adventure with all that money. They've been apart too long, and school is boring. And I won't get off their backs about going to school, their clothes, their music, the kids they're hanging out with, and the same old shit.

They come out of the house that afternoon while I am weeding the garden, standing side by side on the patio, a fat Army surplus pack on each of their backs. Amanda rolls a cigarette between her fingers, then puts it between her black lips and lights it with a yellow Bic. Stephanie's hair is gelled into spikes; dark eyeliner circles her eyes. A coffee mug is tied to each of their packs with twine; Amanda has a pair of Chuck Taylor shoes tied on, as well.

I set the weeds on the ground and brush off my shirt. I walk over to them. "Where are you going?"

"To coffee," Amanda says.

"You need an extra pair of shoes to go to coffee?"

She shrugs, and the two of them slip out of the gate. Several feet behind, I follow to the corner and watch my daughters walk down the street. Toward the bus station, toward town, toward a way of being in the world that is foreign to me. I could go in and call the police, but I know that will do no good. I could jump in the car and chase them. But I don't. This time, I let them go.

Tia Tata

Flor Fernandez Barrios

As a young woman, the prospect of having children was not high on my list of priorities. I was more interested in pursuing my professional goals and becoming a world traveler. My mother complained frequently about the absence of grandchildren in the family, but by the time I turned thirty, she had stopped bringing up the subject of *los nietos.*

To a Cuban woman like my mother, whose entire life was dedicated to her home and raising a family, it was almost impossible to comprehend my decision. I remained an enigma to her and to all her friends. It was often hard to ignore their expectation that I should simply start having babies. When my brother had his first child, Danielle, I felt the world had been lifted from my shoulders. Four years later, my nephew, Esteban, was born, and we became a happy, but more importantly, "normal" Cuban family.

But I was not completely off the hook. With the arrival of these beautiful children came the understanding that I had taken on a new and serious role, that of a "good aunt." Not that anyone handed me a written contract. It was more of a silent agreement, very well defined within the boundaries of my culture. Of course, I didn't mind the task of becoming *Tia Tata* ("Tata" is a family nickname). I truly loved my brother's children. What I didn't anticipate was how deeply my life would be changed by their presence.

When Danielle was six years old and Esteban was two, my brother divorced. His former wife moved to Mexico, leaving her children behind. Danielle and Esteban went to live with my parents in Los Angeles, and my role as their Tia Tata quickly evolved. Though I lived in Seattle, I made sure that Danielle and Esteban knew and felt I was there for them. I called them daily and visited them frequently. I even helped them with their homework over the phone, spending endless hours on math and science projects. I took them to all the "destination" theme parks—Disneyland, Knott's Berry Farm, Magic Mountain. In the summers, I brought them to the Pacific Northwest, where they could enjoy the beauty of nature and attend outdoor camps.

As Danielle and Esteban reached adolescence, we went from playing Monopoly and Uno to having serious conversations about culture, race, spirituality, and life in general. There were also some difficult exchanges when Tia Tata was forced to set limits and to say no to the request for a new CD or one more pair of shoes. I wanted to teach my niece and nephew our family values and help them develop an appreciation for the nonmaterial world. And, sometimes, I couldn't resist noting the contrast between America and the country I left when I was fourteen.

"Oh, no, Tia Tata! Not another lecture about how the families in Cuba don't have anything to eat," Danielle would say before I had a chance to pitch my guilt trip.

"Tia, we are not in Cuba!" Esteban would remind me.

With great reluctance, they accepted my decisions, but not without letting me know how they felt: "Carlos's father bought him a new Nintendo," or "Genie has those shoes. Please, please, can't we buy them?" It was a challenge not to give in to their pleas. I tried very hard not to overly compensate for the absence of their mother with gifts and toys. But all my years as a psychotherapist did not help me keep a completely clear head when it came to my nephew and niece. Every time they cried with me about their mother not calling them, or not visiting them, it simply broke my heart! I was transformed into a mother bear. I wanted to charge down to Mexico, find that woman, and tell her what a selfish creature she was. But in truth, I was hurt that all my love couldn't heal the children's wounds.

With the teenage years came many changes and many challenges. When Esteban turned twelve, he decided he would come for his summer visit alone, without Danielle. He felt he was old enough to adventure on his own. I took this opportunity to do more of what Esteban called "guy things." With that in mind, one day, I pulled out a couple of fishing rods from my basement. I went to the local outdoor store and refilled my tackle box with plenty of hooks, weights, and bait.

I was excited about the prospect of teaching Esteban how to fish. I forgot, though, that these days, boys have a preference for intense stimuli, usually in the form of video games. I believe that Esteban appreciated my efforts, but he was bored. Fishing is a sport that requires patience. It takes time to convince the smart fish to die for a simple night crawler. And that day at Lake Washington, the fish did not appear to be hungry at all. Esteban, used to the thrill of Nintendo, became impatient.

"Tia Tata, I don't think the fish like this bait," he said as he reeled the line back into the spool.

I handed him a fresh worm. He frowned in disgust as he took the wiggling crawler in his fingers.

After three hours of frustration, tangled lines, and lost hooks, I was ready to scream. Instead of paying attention to his fishing rod, Esteban talked incessantly about his video games. I couldn't concentrate on my own fishing. *Shut up!* I wanted to tell him. *You are scaring off the fish!* Finally, as I was getting ready to pack up and drive home empty-handed, Esteban caught his first fish.

I'll never forget the huge smile on my nephew's face as he proudly lifted his catch—a small perch—in the air to be photographed. Esteban was eager to keep fishing, and I was able to teach him a few tricks. When the day ended, we had a bucketful of fish. Better than that, Esteban had forgotten all about his Nintendo. As the sun faded, we watched quietly as the golden aura of the sunset reflected on the lake. I looked across to a stand of old-growth forest at the water's edge. Gleaming in the soft light of dusk, a tall cedar reminded me of the wisdom and healing power of Mother Nature. Somehow, the fishing experiment had worked.

Soon after Esteban returned to California, Danielle arrived for a short visit over Labor Day weekend. At seventeen, she was far more interested in hanging out with her friends at the mall than she was in coming to Seattle to be with her aunt. At first, I was disappointed to hear that her visit would be so brief. I had a mild case of nostalgia, thinking of our annual trips to the rustic summer cabin on Harstene Island. But, believe me, it did not take long to be jolted out of my reverie.

Danielle walked off of the plane wearing a skintight blouse and a jean skirt that accentuated her Latina curves. She had become a stunning young woman seemingly overnight. The next morning, as soon as Danielle opened her eyes and before I had a chance to take a sip from my coffee, she reminded me of my promise to take her shopping at the mall for back-to-school clothes. She sat by my side at the kitchen table and proceeded to tell me her list: a skirt, a jean jacket, a pair of boots . . .

"Danielle, sweetie, I'm waking up."

"I'm sorry, Tia Tata, I'm just so excited about getting new clothes! Last night, I dreamed about the boots. I really want that style with the spiky, tall heels. And do you want me to tell you about the . . ."

"Danielle," I interrupted, "I need to have some coffee first."

Our trip to Nordstrom was a total disaster. Danielle has a Jennifer Lopez look—which is a blessing or a curse, depending on which side of the cultural fence you are on. For Danielle, it was unfortunately more like torture every time she tried on the pencil-thin sizes in the juniors' department. She couldn't find a decent pair of jeans or a single top that fit her. She kept me running back and forth from the dressing room to the floor to get her different sizes. She told me that she definitely did not want the Nordstrom shopping assistant to help her.

"Tia," she cried, "look at her! She is your typical Barbie doll. How could she possibly understand what I need? My boobs are triple her size! And look at my hips, so wide and round. And my big belly . . . " Her voice trailed off as she turned to face the mirror again, her face creasing.

"I don't think you should compare your body to hers," I said in an effort to comfort her. "Look, *mija*, if you were living in Mexico or in Cuba, you would not have to deal with this problem. You know, Latin woman have curves and big buttocks. Nordstrom would go broke in the Caribbean islands! Women are rounder there. They have flesh!"

Of course, telling this to Danielle didn't help. Not at all. She looked at me with teary eyes and shook her head angrily. "Tia, don't you get it? We don't live in Mexico or Cuba. We live in *this* country. Don't you see the ads on television? Don't you go to the movies? Everywhere you turn, you see those skinny women. My God, Tia, wake up!" And with this she grabbed a skirt from my hands and threw it on the floor.

"Come on, let's go home!" She hurriedly put her own clothes back on.

I took a glance at the sad pile of discarded outfits. My heart ached for Danielle. I couldn't bring myself to ask her to try on one more piece of clothing. I hated to see my beloved niece feel so distraught, and I hated Nordstrom for catering only to the tall and thin. The message was clear to everyone: Just go and starve yourself!

Danielle walked ahead of me in silence. I caught up with her and suggested we go have lunch somewhere on the way home. Danielle stomped furiously down the escalator. Then she turned around and, totally oblivious to the people streaming by, looked at me with tears running down her face. "Tia," she said, "I need to stop eating for a month. Maybe then I would be able to fit into those clothes."

I began to tell her that starving herself was not the answer, but I held my tongue. We returned to the car, and I decided to drive out to Alki, a beachfront neighborhood with spectacular views of the sea and mountains. I hoped the cool breeze from the bay would calm her down. But matters got worse. The walking path along the water was crowded with more thin girls and their roller skates. We hadn't even gotten out of the car when Danielle began to sob.

"See, Tia? That's what I mean. Take a look at those girls!"

"Danielle, I see those girls, but . . . " I paused and thought about what I wanted to say. "They have a different body. You are a Latina, my love . . . "

"Stop, Tia! Don't say anything else. I am sick and tired of hearing that Latina number. I tell you, I wish I had blond hair, blue eyes, and long legs, like that girl." Danielle pointed across the street to an athletic-looking young woman stretching her legs. "She looks like a model!"

"Yes," I said, and I felt a wave of sadness sweep over me.

"Look, Tia, I know you want to make me feel good, but . . . all that therapist talk is not helping. I am the one who has to deal with the fact that the boys in my school are not a bit interested in me. They go for those girls, the ones with skinny bodies!"

I had parked the car in the first empty space I found, facing the water. I wanted to say so many things to Danielle, but instead I found myself wordless. I held tight to the wheel. The waters of Puget Sound were serene. A large ferry headed from Vashon Island to downtown Seattle was moving slowly across the bay. There are times when it is best to stay quiet and simply allow the pain to ooze from the wound. Such was the case with Danielle. There was nothing I could say to my beloved child to help ease her grief.

Danielle grew silent.

"Come on, Danielle. Let's go and have some lunch."

I was relieved when she stepped out of the car and joined me. As we walked toward the restaurant, I admired the lovely color of her skin. It was the color of bronze and had the smoothness of velvet. I thought about how many women in Seattle would love such a natural tan. Danielle was such a beautiful young woman. I brooded about the women I had treated over the years in the course of my work. So many of them were incredibly pretty but found themselves ugly when in front of the mirror. Regardless of how thin they were, it was never thin enough.

No matter how much I loved Danielle, I couldn't ease the pain of her suffering right now. I didn't need a crystal ball to predict the agony of her attempts to lose weight. The Atkins diet, the South Beach diet, who knew how many diets she'd try before she turned twenty? And I couldn't deny the fact that though Danielle was Latina, she lived in the United States of America.

The waitress sat us by the window, where we could have a view of the Sound. I looked at Danielle, her eyes still red from crying. I felt a squeezing pain in my heart. I reached over and held her hand.

"Danielle, sweetie, I am sorry."

"Thanks. I'm sorry, too, about giving you such a hard time at the store. I don't know what happened to me. I hate those mirrors."

"I hate them, too, Danielle. Every time I go in there, I am made aware of all my cellulite. Sometimes I wish I could figure out the right size just by looking at it. And those 'personal assistants,' they're like a flock of crows!"

Danielle suddenly giggled, and I joined in. When our orders arrived, we ate our lunch and Danielle brought me up to date on the latest gossip. Julito, the son of Carlos, the man who owns the Cuban market, married his pregnant girlfriend. Luisa is going to Ecuador for Christmas. And wouldn't you know? Mary, the daughter of a distant cousin, came out as a lesbian and is living with her partner.

"I knew it!" Danielle said. "Last time Mary visited us, she brought her 'friend' with her. Grandma didn't believe me when I told her they were more than friends."

"How did you know?" I was surprised by Danielle's openness about a subject that was very taboo in the family.

"Tia, I could tell by the way they were looking at each other."

AFTER DANIELLE FLEW home, I was left to think about her upcoming year at high school, the unbearable peer pressure to be skinny, to fit in. I hadn't even gotten to our talk about birth control and sexually transmitted diseases! And I reflected upon my time with Esteban. How much easier it had been to disentangle fishing line than to attempt to unravel the complex world of a young woman. I wished resolving the situation with Danielle was as simple as it had been to teach Esteban how to unfasten his line and sinker from the rocks at the bottom of the lake.

A few days later, while I was walking the forest trails of a city park along the lake, I came face to face with a magnificent old cedar. While standing by its wide trunk, I felt the strength and comfort emanating from its center. It was then that I understood the nature of a different kind of parenting, one of absolute receptivity.

I sat on the ground with my back against the Mother Cedar, and I thought of my role as Tia Tata in the years ahead. I wanted Danielle and Esteban to experience my presence as a tall and strong tree that could hold them and support them during the difficult moments. It was inevitable that their fishing lines would become entangled many times throughout their lives. All I could promise was to be there, always.

The Girlfriend Sleeps Over

Joyce Maynard

I STILL REMEMBER THE shame I experienced when my breasts began developing and the embarrassment I felt at the prospect of asking my mother for my first bra. I put it off for half a year—months in which I raced to the girls' locker room as fast as I could on gym days so I could secure a bathroom stall to change in. I couldn't bear for the other girls to see my undershirt.

A year later, at fourteen, when I got my period, I was once again struck dumb by the prospect of telling my mother, and so I pedaled my bike to the drugstore and filled my shopping basket with a bunch of unnecessary sundries, all to mask the real purpose of my mission: buying sanitary napkins. Taking out my money to pay, I cringed at the thought of the cashier imagining me menstruating. I would always choose a woman for my cashier. It was still bad enough.

Given the level of shame I felt over everything to do with my body and sex, it is a source of some amazement that I got to the point, only nine years later, of conceiving and bearing a child of my own. One thing I knew when the day came that I had a daughter myself (and then two sons): I wanted my children to grow up with a very different attitude toward their sexuality than what I'd known as a kid. I was going to raise children who wouldn't feel, as I did, that there was something shameful about their bodies. My children would be able to ask questions about sex, and when they did, they'd get straight answers.

Of course, if I was truly to succeed in raising children who felt comfortable with their sexuality, I knew it would take more than words to get the idea across. And we were tested early. It's a totally natural impulse for a four-year-old to put his hand on his crotch for a little pleasure or simply comfort, and the enlightened parent knows she shouldn't tell her son or daughter there's anything wrong in that. But see what happens when he engages in innocent, joyful exploration of his body at the library story hour, or when a neighbor (the minister's wife) stops by your house with a basket of her fresh-picked tomatoes at the precise moment your son is engaging in his joyful exploration. There I was: suddenly suggesting alternative activities for my four-year-old. Taking out the Play-Doh. Setting a bowl of Goldfish crackers on the table. Finger food . . .

Still, I'd like to think that more often than not, the messages conveyed by my children's father and me (long divorced, but of like minds—on this topic, anyway) to our three kids as they grew up were ones that taught them to feel good about themselves, not ashamed. I didn't flaunt my naked body, but neither did I go to excessive lengths to conceal it. When a pregnancy occurred, or a birth, we discussed how that came about—a circumstance that no doubt explains the report we later got from our daughter's pre-school teacher, that our daughter (at age four) was graphically enacting childbirth scenes, complete with moans of pain, during recess time.

When people talk about kids and sex, the focus goes invariably to the teenage years, but of course the way a child views sexuality at fourteen and sixteen is shaped by the signals we give her at two and four and six. I wanted those messages to speak of acceptance, ease, and a certain wholesome recognition that the vast topics of the body, of reproductive biology, and of sex were interesting, worth-while, and healthy. This is a tall order in a culture that identifies the territory, very early on, as shocking, titillating, and unmentionable.

We always used the real names, not cute diminutives, for body parts. Young as they were, our kids understood early that those words carried a certain kind of power. I remember a day, during a family trip to New York City, when my daughter was eight and her younger brothers four and two. We were riding a city bus when Willy, the youngest, decided to make up a song whose much-repeated refrain featured the word "vagina." I suggested that he lower his voice but, not wanting to convey any negative attitudes where female anatomy was concerned, didn't silence him alto-gether. Our fellow passengers gave us stony looks the whole ride uptown. When we reached our stop and I moved toward the door, one woman shook her head at me and said, "You should be ashamed of yourself."

I wasn't. I understood well enough, and tried to convey as much to my kids, that the rules for how things were out in the world and how we needed to behave there were not necessarily the same as how things were in our own family.

Like every little boy I've ever met, mine loved and were endlessly amused by their penises. We lived in rural New Hampshire on a dead-end road, where major entertainment could always be provided for my sons in the form of making designs in the snow while they peed. On hot summer days, our kids played naked in the pond beside our house, and afterward smeared each other's bodies with mud till it dried in the sun, then jumped in the water again to wash the mud off. All three were early, natural sensualists. I believe that's what every child is born to be, until society, or culture, or kindergarten teachers, or television and too many video games, saps it out of them.

PERHAPS ONE ELEMENT that contributed to the almost crackling sense of sexuality around our household during those years—and beyond—came from the fact that I was a single parent. And though I hardly carried on what anybody could have described as a wild social life, a child grows up differently when his mother is dating than he might if she is simply, safely, married off to his dad.

I didn't flaunt my relationships when I had them, and, except for a couple of times when a relationship had reached a level of seriousness that allowed me to believe it might become a permanent one, boyfriends didn't sleep over at our house. Still, over the many years of my single days, my children witnessed no small amount of dating and courtship activity.

One Friday evening—my children having been picked up by their father to spend two nights with him—I was preparing to go off for the weekend with a boyfriend. Suddenly, I heard the door open downstairs and footsteps on the stairs. Next thing I knew, Willy (now ten) had burst in the door to my room, having returned home unexpectedly to pick up a crucial piece of sports equipment. He thought he'd give me a kiss goodbye. When he entered the room, I was in my underwear—the kind a woman might save for a weekend away with a man.

He looked at me sharply. "What's the point of having purple underwear if nobody ever sees it?" my son asked. But I understood what he was saying, really. That he was afraid somebody would.

I LIKE TO THINK that among the many difficulties of growing up in a single-parent household, one positive element was my sons' acquisition of an unusually keen sensitivity toward women. As uncomfortable as it must have been for my children, growing up with a mother who was, herself, struggling through some of the things more typically experienced in adolescence (like wishing you had a date for the dance), the experience gave them a level of compassion and openness they might not otherwise have achieved. Because I had no steady, ongoing partner through the years, my sons recognized, more swiftly than boys whose father was in residence might, the need to offer not simply physical assistance, for things like cleaning up the kitchen or shoveling snow, but a certain amount of understanding and sympathy, too. There was the night one winter— my sons around eleven and thirteen—when I headed out, dateless, to a local dance without having realized that if ever there were a night I'd be unlikely to find unattached dance partners, February 14 would top the list. So, I returned home about fifteen minutes later and collapsed in tears on our living room couch, where my sons had sprawled, watching an action video.

"Everyone else had a boyfriend," I wept.

Willy rubbed my neck. Charlie stroked my hair. No doubt their sister would have said something comforting, too, but she was out. (At a dance, in fact. *She* had a date.)

"If I was one of those boyfriends, I would have left my girlfriend to dance with you, Mom," Willy said.

Charlie concurred.

I put on a record then—Louis Armstrong—and the three of us danced.

OVER THE YEARS of raising three children as a single parent, I had abundant opportunity to test my commitment to the honesty approach where matters of sexuality and the body were concerned: There was the time my son walked in on a boyfriend and me, kissing on the couch. And the time when one of them, hearing about the phenomenon of oral sex, asked if I knew anyone who actually did that. And when one of my sons found my vibrator and asked what it was. As uncomfortable as it was, every time I gave my children a straight answer to a straight question, it got a little easier. And I like to think that it made them feel freer to ask their questions, and freer, too, to speak honestly of their own experiences.

My daughter was the first to reach adolescence. She had a boyfriend—and then another—but my strongest image of her teenage years is not so much of Audrey entwined with a boy as it is of Audrey surrounded by a large and boisterous crowd of friends. Our house was often where they gathered: up in her room, listening to music, and it never seemed all that surprising when I'd wake up the next morning to find that a whole bunch of kids had slept over. I can remember countless times when I'd come into my daughter's room in the morning to find two or three kids of both sexes stretched out on the floor and another three or four (along with Audrey) on the bed. The whole thing had the feeling of a campout sleepover, and specifically because there were so many kids around all the time, it seemed pretty clear that whatever was going on in my daughter's room, sex was not a part of the story.

My sons were just fourteen and twelve when their older sister left home for college and I entered what I think of now, looking back, as the second phase of my parenting life: Boy World. It's no big surprise—given their level of exposure to the not-particularly-well-concealed vulnerabilities of women (one in particular) and the unusual access they'd been given to the lives of at least two well-loved female figures—that at an early age, my sons developed a certain reputation among girls.

Girls have always loved my sons. It didn't hurt that they were handsome and funny. But above all, they were kind. More than once, my eldest son, Charlie, would find himself the lone boy invited to an all-girl party. When my younger son, Willy, turned thirteen, he began buying flowers for girls he liked. Just one flower, but it would be a rose. At fourteen, Willy came home one day with one of those little recipe books they sell at the supermarket checkout counter—*Romantic Italian Dinners*—and announced he was inviting a girl over, for whom he intended to cook a meal. He set the table with a white cloth that night, stuck a candle in an old wine bottle, and bought sparkling grape juice. The meal was pasta with homemade spaghetti sauce and tiramisu. I made a point that evening of going upstairs early to watch a movie, but I could hear the music he'd selected as the accompaniment for the meal. Pachelbel's *Canon in D*.

EVEN IN THEIR EARLY teens, my sons seemed drawn to have not simply girlfriends but relationships. Willy was the kind to talk on the phone for hours—so long, in fact, that I would sometimes come into his room late and find him conked out, with the receiver still off the hook on the pillow beside him and humming the sound of a dial tone.

In his junior year, Charlie fell in love with a young woman I will call Emily. It was a beautiful relationship to observe—full of tenderness and excitement and romance, genuine consideration for each other, and a great deal of communication. Because Emily lived some distance from our house (on the other side of the Golden Gate Bridge from our house in Marin County), the pattern developed that if they were out together late, one of them would simply stay over at the home of the other, on whichever side of the bridge they ended up. When Emily would sleep at our house, I'd set out blankets and a towel for her on the futon in the TV room, and the next morning, I'd cook French toast or pancakes for us all and think how wonderful it was to have a girl around again, wishing she could be with us more often.

This was a time in which my own romantic life was pretty bleak.

No man in the picture, none on the horizon. Looking across the breakfast table some mornings, at the two young seventeen-year-olds so much in love, I felt a certain wistfulness.

As a mother who had dedicated herself to presenting sex as a natural and healthy part of life, I tried to convey to my sons my willingness to talk about whatever issues might come up in their lives. Sometimes, too, it seemed as though I should not simply wait for them to raise a concern (which can be hard, as I remembered well from my days of changing into my gym suit in the toilet stall), but to go ahead and address it.

In that spirit, I bought a box of condoms and set it in my sons' bathroom with the explanation that while I thought they were too young to be sexually active, I also recognized that they might feel otherwise and that I could not ultimately control their choices.

"One thing's for sure," I said. "If you're going to be sexually active, you'd better be sure you're both protected." Physical protection being only a part of the story; there was all that other stuff that goes on, too, about the heart. Didn't I know?

ONE SATURDAY MORNING, following a Friday night in which Charlie and Emily had ended up together on our side of the bridge, I fired up my frying pan to make the pancakes and headed downstairs to my sons' rooms to wake them up—the two of them, plus Emily. Only this time, when I walked through the den to get to their rooms, there was nobody on the futon. When I got to Charlie's room, I saw two heads sticking out from under the covers. Charlie's being one. Emily's the other.

At the time, I didn't say anything, besides calling out breezily that breakfast was ready. But after Emily had gone home, I went back downstairs, where my sons were installed, and told them we had to talk.

"It's this sleeping-over business," I said. "Just because Emily gets to sleep at our house doesn't mean it's okay for her to sleep in your *bed*, Charlie."

He looked at me sweetly. "We like to snuggle, Mom," he said. "What's wrong with that?"

Nothing, of course. Who could come down on the side against snuggling? Particularly when the person being snuggled was someone as lovable as Emily. Wouldn't I have liked it—a whole lot—if I had someone great to snuggle with, myself?

"But it's not just snuggling, Charlie," I told him. "That's just not possible between a teenage boy and girl who are crazy about each other. It's going to lead to sex, of course. That's pretty well unavoidable."

My son didn't deny it. He just looked at me.

"So," I said. Faltering, before I'd even begun. Being the authority figure with the heavy boot is my least favorite part of parenthood. "From now on, the rule around here is no girlfriends sleeping in bed with you." There. I said it. This was the kind of thing the sensible, grown-up parents said.

"So, let's get this straight," said Willy. "Charlie is only allowed to have sex in cars?"

This didn't sound like a very good bottom-line conclusion. But neither had I arrived at a better one. I opened my mouth to try again, not even sure of what would come out next.

"When someone sleeps over with you this way," I began, "it involves the whole family in a way. That might not be fair to the rest of us."

"What about when you had a boyfriend and he slept over?" Willy again. "Maybe we weren't always so comfortable with that, either."

There was a statement that had a ring of guilt-inspiring truth.

"And anyway, we all like Emily, right?" my younger son went on. "And it's not like she's some person none of us knows, who just showed up at the breakfast table." At this point, in fact, Charlie and Emily had been going together in a pretty serious way for more than a year. Longer than any relationship I'd had since their father and I had parted ten years earlier (though my sons were too kind to point this out).

"I thought you said we shouldn't be embarrassed or shy," my four-teen-year-old pointed out. "Like, what's so terrible about expressing affection?"

"It's just that sex is . . . sex is . . . sex is . . . private," I said. "Sex is something you do when you're independent enough to have your own place to live. Not something you get into in your own home, with your family all around."

Long pause again. My older son, whose actions had inspired this discussion, still said nothing, but his younger brother demonstrated no such reticence.

"Hmmm," he reflected, wrinkling his brow. "Let me just make sure I've got this clear. Does this policy about not doing it in our own house apply to masturbation, too?"

. . . .

As I said, I believe in talking straight with one's children—using the real words for real things, communicating openly, and, when we do, conveying to our kids the clear message that their sexuality is a natural and healthy part of life. Free from guilt and shame. Encouraging the asking of questions and giving straight answers in return.

It was my children's job, as teenagers in love, to lobby with all their hearts and their best debating skills (including a certain below-the-belt impulse to inspire massive guilt in their mother) for the right to have their girlfriends sleep over. And it was probably my job, as their parent, to say no.

Nonetheless, sometime over the course of the next few months, Emily began sleeping over regularly at our house on weekends. Or at least, if she didn't, it was only because Charlie was sleeping over—in similarly close proximity—at her house.

And when, a couple of years later, my younger son embarked on his own equally serious relationship, also at age sixteen, there came a point when his girlfriend, too, started sleeping over, no longer on the futon. While, two floors above, I continued to sleep alone.

And though I like to think of myself as a woman who considers carefully the meaning and significance of her choices as a parent and comes to them with resolute conviction, I cannot say that—in the matter of the girlfriends sleeping over—any of these outcomes occurred as the result of some carefully thought out moral position, or that my ultimate stance on the matter was one of utter and unwavering clarity. Our lives simply evolved, and that's the direction things went.

. . . .

A FEW YEARS BACK, I published a memoir about my life. In it, I told a number of fairly intimate stories about my experiences. This book was hugely criticized at the time of its publication. Interestingly, a very particular theme emerged in the negative remarks that were made, less about the book than about me, personally. I was seldom criticized for my writing style, or charged with a failure to portray interesting situations and characters. A single word showed up, again and again, in the invective leveled at my work. The word was "shameless."

As much as I differed with their ultimate assessment of my work, I knew my critics were right about me. I had come a long way from that awkward girl in the locker room stall. I *was* shameless. And, with any luck, my children would grow up to be that way, too. All evidence suggested they were headed in that direction.

During this period in which I was branded the shameless woman, the youngest of my children left home. Willy, the boy who once serenaded vaginas on a New York City bus, years before most of us ever heard of Eve Ensler, had become one of the most fearless and self-confident people I've ever met. Willy—now Will—went to Africa for a year, on his own. Months would go by in which I'd receive only the barest forms of communication from my seventeen-year-old, with weeks of silence between each message. Then I'd receive e-mails that might begin and end with lines like, "I'm over the malaria now. Love, Will."

And so I was alone then. Nobody around to call me on wearing purple underwear. No teenage girlfriends sleeping over anymore, either.

When the last child leaves, as Will did, there comes the day of reckoning, at last—the moment when a parent looks back over the tangle of years that once seemed endless, and now appear so fleeting, and considers how the whole thing went. Where her regrets lie. What she'd do differently now. And what may actually have worked.

It's dangerous, allowing oneself to feel smug about any of this. I don't subscribe to the practice some parents engage in when their children reach their twenties and all appearances suggest they're doing great—namely, patting oneself on the back and saying, "Look at my kids. They turned out great. Here's how I did it."

No one in this family is hooked on heroin. When my children sign off on their—infrequent—phone calls to me, they say, "I love you," and when they come home, which they do now and then, they still give me not just a hug but a kiss. But I'm not about to start proclaiming that I've got some kind of recipe for successful parenting here.

Still, where attitudes about sex are concerned (and, I'll dare to say it, attitudes about love, as well), I'll venture to say I see promising signs of health and well-being among my offspring. My children may or may not make happy marriages, raise healthy children, build careers they love, contribute in a lasting way to the welfare of society. Not one of them has a regular nine-to-five kind of job at the moment (neither has either of their parents, hardworking as we've been these past three decades), and none has much of a savings account, I think. But to me, getting this other part figured out is a different kind of money in the bank, and so it makes me happy that in the last six months, each of their current partners has written me a note or called, simply to thank me for my extraordinarily loving daughter or son.

I can hardly accept credit for this. Except to say, my children grew up unafraid to speak of the unmentionable things (sex high on the list) that are the facts of all our lives. It strikes me that there can be little better foundation for healthy coupling than the ability to communicate free of guilt or shame. To say what we think, and ask for what we need, and express how we feel, free of ambivalence or hang-ups. In short, to be shameless. Which might even allow a person to say, in answer to a question concerning the reason for wearing purple underwear, "Yes, somebody may see it, perhaps." Because what, when you think about it, is so terrible about that?

Gods and Monsters

Marion Winik

She was so deeply imbedded in my consciousness that for the first year of school I seem to have believed that each of my teachers was my mother in disguise. As soon as the last bell had sounded, I would rush off for home, wondering as I ran if I could possibly make it to our apartment before she had succeeded in transforming herself. Invariably, she was already in the kitchen by the time I arrived, setting out my milk and cookies. Instead of causing me to give up my delusions, however, the feat merely intensified my respect for her powers.

—*Philip Roth,* Portnoy's Complaint

EVERYBODY KNOWS WHAT a monstrous emotional burden it is to have a mother. Whether the mommy in question is angelic, asphyx-iating, absent, or just annoying, it is the task of the child to endure her, escape her, then explain her, to unload her like containerized cargo, perhaps in therapy. In our child-centric culture, we see the relationship from one direction, as if the child were the living thing and the mother something tremendously powerful yet insensate, like the ocean, or the weather.

But this high-pressure system I'm in right now is hardly barometric. As the mother of two teenagers from my first marriage (I was widowed in my mid thirties) and a toddler from my current one, I am experiencing simultaneously two phases that really should be separated by a decent interval: the wild tumble of falling in love with a baby and the bewildering pain of living with adolescents. As I respond to my daughter's dependence on me with passion that is no less fearsome for being evolutionarily ordained, I'm also coping with my sons' break for the fence. Sure, growing up is tough. But check out this bad love affair from my point of view, and you tell me who's being scarred for life.

To my three-year-old, Jane, I am the world, I am God, and I am love incarnate. She can barely stand to let me out of her sight. She cries my name as soon as she wakes up and any time we are separated. She lights up like Las Vegas at my reappearance, often leaping into the air with joy. There is almost nothing I cannot fix with my embrace, very little she prefers to my attention—sorry, Dora the Explorer, but it isn't even close—and she showers me with positive reinforcement at regular intervals. "You're such a good helper, Mommy," she tells me when I hand her the toilet paper. "That's beautiful," she says when I put on a pink shirt. "I lub you," she reminds me every hour or so, in case I have forgotten, sometimes racing into the room and shouting it as she flies past me, sturdy legs churning, dark-blond tresses flying, urgent in her errand as a medieval messenger.

I am not the only person to bask in the love-light of this little love machine. She adores her father, whom she calls "Honey" with imperial confidence. She responds to her older brothers and sister (my husband has two kids from a previous marriage who live with us on weekends) with pure delight. But I am Mommy, and I am number one. What do you expect? The germ of her was stored inside me since my own birth, she waxed like the moon in my belly, for eighteen months she took her food from my body. To say I am her favorite means little in such a rigged competition, I know, but I am.

It's not like it's the first time this has happened to me. I remember the infancy of my son Hayes, now sixteen, as one long, golden afternoon, a swoon of nursing and cuddling and staring into his big dark eyes, the ceiling fan spinning overhead and Dream Academy playing in the background. I had lost a baby, a full-term stillbirth, less than a year before he was born. Hayes washed over me like morphine for a person mangled, lying in the woods, waiting for medical assistance for quite a while. Then, a couple of years later, Vincie came, so charismatic and radiant we called him the baby messiah.

But Jane is the last, and I know she's the last, and I thought I would never do this again, I thought I would have sons but never a daughter. My sweet little girl, my beauty, my Nooza Pooza, my fountain of love. Even as struggle and irritation find their way into my responses, even as she learns to say *No* and *Get my shoes!* and to whine and hound *Mommy this Mommy that Mommy Mommy MOMMY!*—I am stunned to realize how connected, how consumed, how converted to a tool for her use I have become.

(Again!) *If anything were to happen to her,* I think once or twice a day, and stop myself right there.

And something *is* going to happen to her, even if none of my worst fears comes to pass, and she grows normally to adolescence. At that point, I can expect to have precisely the inverse experience of the festival of love I am enjoying now. Torn from my pedestal like a statue of Saddam Hussein, I will be rejected as powerfully as I was once embraced. For just as a toddler is devoted to cathecting you, a twelve-year-old uses all the force of his particular being to tear free.

With emotionally muffled Hayes, it was a quiet junta, a revolution of rocky sullenness. He responded to less than a quarter of the conversation I directed to him, and to that fraction with icy rebuff or curled-lip scorn. The idea, it seemed, was that I would wait on him hand and foot while staying entirely out of his way, requiring nothing of him, and completely avoiding all public and private displays of affection. The summer he was twelve, I remember, my mother asked him why he was being so mean to me. He replied simply, "Because I hate her."

With the more passionate Vince, things have been livelier. At late-eleven, when it began, he once seemed about to literally explode with rage because I asked him to put the ketchup on the table (a few dozen times), then accidentally bumped into him in front of the fridge while he was finally complying. This past year, seventh grade—watch out, my friends, for seventh grade—it got much worse. He cursed at me, he screamed at me, he ordered me to shut up and leave him alone; I was without question the worst thing that happened to him on any given day.

In the preposterously rainy spring of this benighted year, it came to pass that Vince was not doing his homework, his grades were dropping, and thus a scheme was inaugurated where the guidance counselor and I were both to sign off on an assignment sheet he completed every day. One afternoon, I asked him several times to see the sheet, and instead of answering me, he left the kitchen and went to his room. A bit later, I was up there knocking and asking him to show it to me—little Jane was right beside me; I was on my way to take her to the bathroom, I think—and finally he responded: "Go away! Just go away!" Stubbornly, I did not. So he came out on the landing and stuck his face in my face and put his hand on my chest and shoved me, and he said, "Fuck you, you dirty bitch."

My response to this was more profound and less coherent than anger. I struggled to breathe. For three days, I would find tears welling up in my eyes on and off, every time I thought of it. I could barely speak to him. Yet, the infraction seemed virtually past punishment. When, the previous summer, he and a friend had semi-accidentally set fire to a neighbor's hayfield, I grounded him for a month. But what to do about this? Take away his screen name? *Talk to him,* I asked his stepfather, and I believe he tried. Finally, there was an apology of some sort, followed by a conversation about what it is that makes him blow up like that, about how his explosiveness hurts and even frightens me (though I know what it's like to have a bad temper, actually), about how we could do it better next time. This first, halting conversation was followed by others, and eventually, after he had a contretemps with a teacher at school, I took him to a counselor to talk about dealing with anger. But the fact is, I don't know how to be one of those parents whose child would never dare talk to them this way, and if he did, who would make sure he would never do it again. I know this is a weakness of my parenting, and it is also a strength.

Whatever I did about this incident, what I could not do was turn back the clock. At least for a few terrifying moments, my baby messiah had turned into a demon-child from hell, and he was determined to drive me off.

He has to, right? He has to separate, to break the bonds of my milky mothering, my cloying care. I did it too, so I know, I remember how it was, I remember how I treated my mother—though I stopped somewhere short of "Fuck you, you dirty bitch." Adolescence is poison, it is torture, it is unbelievable frustration. I didn't just hate her, I hated everything, which was her, and to escape her, I wanted to molt my life like snakeskin and wriggle free to some unimaginable other world.

Even if I know this separation is necessary, it breaks my heart. And even if my heart is broken, I can't just skulk off and lick my wounds, because the little infidels still need me to love them, still want that tiny dot in the distance that used to be the whole world to receive them warmly on their occasional visits. All I can do is find some cooler place to stand, some way to let go but not leave, so I can continue the task of caring about people who are conducting a vigorous multi-year exorcism of me.

But for God's sake, do I have to go through both of these things at the same time, the toddler and the adolescents? It is truly insane. It forces me to remember that this boy who cannot tolerate me standing next to him once sucked me in as if I were oxygen. It makes me envision the day my darling lover-girl will see me as the toxic cloud that blocks the sun. I know I'm supposed to accept this as perfectly normal, part of the job and the process, and know that it too will pass. But imagine the indignity: The people you once took baths with, whose very tushies you tenderly cared for, *will not even answer you when you speak.* And nature, that dirty bitch, doesn't make you fall out of love with them the way it does them with you. They see your embrace as a chokehold; to you, it is still an embrace. They see your curiosity as a vile invasion; for you, it is still a natural act of care. And so I teach Jane to cut her food, to ride a bike, to say her phone number and address, knowing full well what I am pushing her toward.

Of course, every day is not the same. Just last week, I spent over an hour chatting amiably with Vince as we bodysurfed together at the beach. Not long from now, they will leave adolescence behind and become fresh-minted grownups, and I will fall in love all over again with these friendly, busy people who carry my whole beating heart in that back jeans pocket sagging below their asses. Then they will move on into their lives and patronize me, remind themselves to call me, brush aside my queries about their classes, their careers, their marriages. They will dread my death, but they will also dread the sound of my voice on the phone, like an old flame who just won't go away.

And like a billion mothers before me, I will make my peace with it. I will play cards, read novels, and make the favorite pie when asked. I will take my crumbs and hide my scars. I will smile a serene and knowing smile when they hand me my grandchildren.

Piece of My Heart

Turn Signals

Louise Erdrich

THREE OF MY FOUR daughters were born in the dead of winter.
One made it to early spring only because she was overdue. So, for
me, the shortest days of the year and the deepest cold are a backdrop to the perilous stories of birth and the radiant exhaustion of
new motherhood. Now that my three oldest daughters are in their
teens, I can add driving to the pleasures and dangers of having children with winter birthdays.

Because the oldest two both took the driver's test the day after
their sixteenth birthdays, much of the practice driving—with
learner's permits, and me riding as the requisite adult passenger—
took place on those slush-ridden, black-iced, snowbound, or low-
visibility Minnesota mornings as we made our way harrowingly to
school. The rite of passage was conducted on the bitterly cold asphalt
of the Golden Valley driver's course. Both daughters passed the test
by one point on their first try—a result recounted with pride and
excitement to a mother who could react only with a terrified gulp.

Then came the big moment: my daughter would stride to the driver's side of the car, pull the door open, slide in, and drive away. Both times, I was unprepared. After all, when they took their first steps, they walked *into*, not out of, my arms. Once the car had rounded the corner of the street and my daughter had disappeared, I'd stand rooted to the boulevard. Inevitably, an unpredicted ice storm would begin a few minutes later. But there was so much to be scared of in addition to the weather—all the reasons that the cost of car insurance for teenagers is astronomical. Not to mention the other drivers. I'd experience a form of parental sorrow that should be endowed with a German portmanteau word, say, *Mutterkinderwinterfahrenschade.*

When I was on the upslope to fifty, I found that I was pregnant again. My due date was, of course, in January. When winter came that year, everything coincided—the novice driving, the hormones (mine and my teenagers'), the wretched ice on the streets, and the gorgeous new snow. The time was fraught with my efforts to let my teens be teens, even as I seemed to be regressing into a shadowland of jitters.

My youngest daughter was born during one of those January thaws when the snow packs low to the earth, exuding a heavy mist that turns a golden peach color under halogen street lamps, and everything is muted in a fog of sunset. On road surfaces, this fog freezes to an unspeakably slick rime that you need crampons to walk on. My baby's father drove his red Dodge pickup ninety miles an hour to get to the hospital. He literally slid all the way down I-94. Everyone was somehow fine.

As we prepared to leave the hospital on a melting, sparkling morning, we realized that my oldest daughter would have to drive me and the baby home. There was no safe place in the truck for a baby seat, and I was not allowed behind the wheel of a car. We put the new baby in the sky-blue minivan we had relied on for years. I rode. The baby slept. I was amazed at it all: our safe, orderly progress, the unhazardous conditions, our processional grandeur as we were guarded from behind by the red Dodge Ram. I had made a surprise loop, it seemed, a double-back maneuver in my life. The ride was momentous, historical, and calm. My daughter's hands on the steering wheel were properly placed at ten o'clock and two o'clock, as she had been taught. The trees were dripping. The street washed dark. We reached home, and the rest of our lives commenced.

It snowed and snowed until the snow seemed permanent. The nights were crazed, the nights were peaceful. There was the radiance and the madness, and now, three years later, another daughter— about to turn sixteen—has begun painting and unpainting her fingernails and performing other mysterious gestational rituals that will culminate, I know from experience, with her rising into the winter light, the day after her birthday, and passing her driver's test by one point. When she drives away, I'll have only the baby left. And when the baby—unthinkable thought—drives away, too, I'll stand on the boulevard for a long time before walking back into the house. Inside, in my old age, I'll take up drinking or knitting or prayer, or perhaps all three at once; I'll produce sacred three-armed sweaters that will at least keep my girls warm on winter roads.

Band of Brothers

Laura Smith Porter

THE DOORBELL RINGS.

"The guys are here," I call to my son as I go to the back door. He's in the den, playing a baseball game on the computer.

Two fifteen-year-old boys are standing on the porch. Each is wearing an electric guitar strapped to his back in a black case and carrying a large amplifier.

"Men," I say to them in my customary greeting.

"Hey," they answer in deep voices that still surprise me.

I have known one of these boys since he was in the first grade, long before he had shaggy hair and braces. He is my son's best friend. The other one, also with long hair but postbraces, has been around only since seventh grade, when he moved to our town. He has always been tall, but in the past couple of months, we have watched him sail well past six feet.

They pause in the hall to kick off sneakers that look as though they could fit a pair of linebackers.

"The boy around?" asks the one with braces.

"On the computer."

They nod and troop through the kitchen, banging the amplifiers against their knees.

The tall one stops.

"Zoë didn't make any cookies, did she?" he asks hopefully. Together, my son and his friends have been known to go through a couple of dozen chocolate chip cookies in one sitting. Before dinner.

"Not yet. She said she was going to."

"Cool," he says.

"Hey, Zoë! How about getting busy on some cookies?" I hear them call out as they pound up the stairs to rock music central, the extra bedroom on the second floor where we have stashed my son's drum set. When the boys are in there with the door shut, we can listen to their renditions of Nirvana's best (or worst, depending upon one's perspective) from downstairs without risking the loss of an eardrum.

My daughter is too far away for me to hear her response to the request for baked goods, but I'm pretty sure she has told them to get lost. At eleven, she is more than able to hold her own with these guys. She basically considers the band a single entity: a three-headed, six-legged brother.

I go into the den. "Max, your friends are here. Don't you think you should go up there?"

He doesn't even look up. "They know I'm here, Mom. Relax."

Sure enough, in five minutes, their footsteps clatter back down the steps and loud voices travel along the hall and into the den, where the three boys greet each other with a series of grunts. The television clicks on, and a chair scrapes. Somebody shuts the door. I can describe the scene without even looking. One boy is on the computer; the other two are on the couch, one holding the remote control for the television and the other the game pad that enables two people to play a computer game at the same time. For the next hour, they will alternate between MVP Baseball and a rapid tour along the television highway, with periodic stops at Comedy Central and MTV. They will emerge only in search of food.

Eventually, they'll remember that they're here for band practice.

WHEN I FIRST realized that I was going to have a son, I had no idea what to expect. An only child, I had grown up in a world of girls. My boy cousins lived across the country; the boys in my class at school were so firmly the Other that my friends and I believed they existed only as an evil counterpart to what we considered our own cleaner, more rational, *better* natures. I didn't begin to have actual male friends until I was in high school, where even the most platonic relationship had a raging undercurrent of hormonal possibility.

By the time I became a mother, I had a far more evolved view of gender differences. In my more sanctimonious prenatal moments, I declared that ours would be a gender-neutral household. After all, I pontificated to anyone who would listen to me, girls and boys were exactly the same. And then came Max. From the start, there was much in him that I recognized: his father's gentle soul and wry humor, my reserve and perfectionism. But I also had to admit that he and I were unmistakably different. When he was two, for instance, he came upon a basket full of tiny pumpkins I had set out for a Halloween party. Surveying them with interest, he reached in and, with lightning speed, fired one after another across the living room to his father, who caught each one without once pausing in his conversation. I knew then that I was in the presence of a force beyond my comprehension.

As Max and his friends have grown up, I have often felt like Jane Goodall observing in the wild. For years, our house was the backdrop for full-pitched LEGO and Playmobil battles, horses and spacemen and knights scattered down the stairs and across the couch cushions. The back of the front door held a basketball hoop; the living room hosted a permanent game until we moved to a larger house and the court moved to Max's bedroom. Wherever we lived, the ceilings never seemed high enough or the furniture strong enough to contain the exuberance of boys who needed to express themselves with full lung capacity and the flexing of every small muscle.

Now that they are teenagers, these large, deep-voiced boys are still as deeply thrilled with anything that makes noise, turns on electronically, or involves rules that can be endlessly debated as they were when they were six. I love their directness with each other, the puppyish way they clown around, and their unlimited capacity to be silly.

Like most parents, I am constantly torn between wanting to watch my children grow up and wanting to keep them small forever. To my surprise, however, I have found myself welcoming Max's adolescence. I know what it was like to be a girl growing up, both physically and emotionally. I remember the self-consciousness and the cringing embarrassments, both large and small; there are enough slammed doors and hot-tempered outbursts in my past to know that I will be getting as good as I gave my own mother when my daughter crosses the great divide. But Max's growing up has taken me into uncharted territory. It took an observation from another mother to tell me that his perennially hoarse voice was actually changing. His sister, giggling at dinner one night, pointed out the little mustache I had thought was dirt. The widening shoulders and the huge feet seem nothing short of miraculous. How can it be possible that the toddler I used to prop on my hip can now pick me up and toss me into the air?

I certainly don't celebrate every sign of his impending adulthood. In recent months, he has developed a mumbling teenage-speak that on occasion produces full paragraphs of completely incomprehensible language. And there are the mood swings. Living with an adolescent boy is like subsisting in an irregular weather pattern: deafening claps of thunder followed immediately by a beatific, cloudless sky.

But most of our interactions are pleasant enough. He isn't locked in his room with the door shut, exploring the dubious world of the Internet. When he is upset about something, he sometimes seeks me out to talk about it. And, because right now his favorite pastime is to play rock music with his friends, we pretty much always know where he is.

WHEN THE GUYS started the band two years ago, they were relatively new musicians. Max had just started playing the drums; one of the guitar players was teaching himself to play using an Internet program. They bought black T-shirts that said I AM A MEMBER OF A PROMISING LOCAL BAND and got together every weekend to crash through what sounded like three or four measures of fifteen different songs. They decorated the band room with a small lamp, a cranberry-colored rug remnant, a three-foot plastic Doric column, and a wooden duck, which they named "The Duck."

Over time, those jam sessions have paid off. Now that they have an actual repertoire, they have been talking about playing in public, maybe at school or—someday—at a dance. Once last fall, they gave an impromptu concert for their parents, allowing us a brief glimpse into their world. Transfixed, we all huddled in the doorway, greedily trying to take in every detail without making it obvious that we were staring. The guitar players curved their long bodies over the necks of the instruments, every strum an assault against the strings. Max, behind them, controlled the beat, the sticks in his hand flashing from crash to high hat. The singer's voice rasped and held, making the words of the White Stripes's "Seven Nation Army" his own. They communicated in quick sidelong glances and abrupt bobs of the head, moving smoothly from one song to the next. None of the adults could quite look at one another, all of us struck simultaneously by the painful twist of memory, the slender hope of what might be. They are babies, our sons; they are men. They are impossibly, heartbreakingly cool.

NOW, ON THIS LATE Saturday afternoon in the spring of their freshman year in high school, the door to the den slams open and into the wall. Loud voices tumble over one another, interrupting with can-you-top-this wisecracks. The clattering, bumping noises in the hall tell me that they are heading toward the kitchen. They cannot ever seem to move from one place to another without colliding with the walls a few times. I think they're still figuring out that they can no longer all fit through a doorway at the same time.

The refrigerator door opens.

"Mom?" Max calls, right on cue. "Do we have anything to eat?"

"I bought stuff for nachos," I answer.

"All right!"

It's the perfect afternoon. They sit around the kitchen downing a huge platter of nachos and large glasses of juice, laugh a lot, get back on the computer and instant message girls, throw grapes at each other, play some Nintendo, go outside for a quick game of Wiffle Ball and, for dessert, blow up marshmallows in the microwave.

I come into the kitchen to find them huddled around the microwave, cheering on the latest marshmallow, which has expanded to roughly eight times its original size.

"Did you guys find enough to eat?"

"Yeah, thanks, Mom."

There is a reverential hush as the giant marshmallow emerges from the microwave and, within seconds, collapses. They groan.

"Let's see what happens if we put in more than one," Max suggests.

"Yeah, try three."

"No, six! Put in six!" Giggling, they stack up a half dozen and set the plate on the turntable.

Zoë comes into the kitchen as they're elbowing one another out of the way to look in the oven window.

"How long are they going to be here?" she whispers to me.

"I don't know. Awhile."

She sighs. "They're so loud." She looks around the kitchen. The cheese-encrusted nacho platter sits on the kitchen table, decorated with splashes of salsa and crumpled napkins. An open bottle of juice sits in a puddle; the cap has dropped on the floor.

"And disgusting. You should make them clean up after themselves."

"You won't think they're so disgusting when you're a little older."

"Gross, Mom. Boys are stupid."

"Ah, man, that's awesome!" The marshmallows have transmogrified into a sticky mass. One of the boys pokes at it with a finger.

"Let's play some music," Max says.

They grab the bag of marshmallows and, muttering their thanks, amble out of the kitchen. Max shoots me a look to see if I've registered his failure to deal with the mess. I have, but wave him away, deciding to let it go for now.

Within minutes, the wail of a guitar riff fills the house, accompanied by a steady rhythm and interspersed with the occasional thud of feet and a shout.

Not much longer now. Just a few more beats, and it will be time for them to move on.

How I will miss them.

Commuting with Rose

Stephen J. Lyons

FOUR O'CLOCK and I arrive to pick up my daughter, Rose, in front of the Moscow, Idaho, public library. She sits on the west-facing stone stairs, the unused entrance to the old Carnegie section that now houses children's books. On the stairs with Rose is Rachel, also of the Moscow High School ("Pride of the North") class of 1998. Here sit two seventeen-year-olds deep in conversation, and school about to end for the year. The weak rays of this spring's on-and-off sun hit their faces and hair in such a way as to warm the coldest heart with youth and promise.

This is May on the Palouse, a tender time when the fat buds of ancient lilac bushes break apart and seduce us with scent. From every distant corner of town, cock pheasants call in their hens and quail offer their high purrs. Finches, mourning doves, and black-capped chickadees compete for birdsong space and nesting sites. Cottonwood flotsam drifts overhead like snow. I feel lazy, almost drowsy, so I sit in the car and drink it all in for a moment, letting the nonsense of the electronic workday evaporate and hoping the girls don't spot me.

I've been picking Rose up at the library after school for years. Most afternoons I find her curled up with a book or magazine in the back room; lately, in these teenage years, she sits close to her boyfriend, John, at a secluded table, sometimes studying and sometimes pretending to study. She is rarely late, always dependable—except for once. Two years ago, on a brilliant Indian summer day, she and John, in the midst of stealing time together, walked out of school after third period to take turns calling in sick from a phone booth, lowering their voices in their best parental imitations, which were as transparent as cellophane to the school secretary.

John's father called me at work with one of those "We have a problem" openers, which means, "I have a problem that involves you and now we have a problem that I expect you to help me solve." John had finally turned up at home and come clean with the whole scam. I found Rose exactly where I knew she would be: at the library, calmly reading. What followed could be classified as an authentic "scene"—a scolding in my fiercest father voice, Rose defiantly denying and then giving in to confession and tears. She said they'd only been drinking coffee at Third Street Market (for four hours!), and besides, school was boring. I sat in front of her, brought those tears right out, gave her an earful about responsibility and truth, and questioned her sudden interest in coffee. (I never mentioned, of course, that I walked out of high school in Chicago my junior year to protest the shootings at Kent State but instead of going to an antiwar rally, I spent the afternoon in the left-field bleachers of Wrigley Field, watching the Cubs lose.)

Nearby, in the library, a young mother carrying her baby in a trendy Mayan wrap glared at me with disapproval. *Just you wait,* I thought. *That cute, cherubic baby sucking on fruit leather will someday carve deep worry wrinkles into your healthy face. It won't even matter if you are a vegetarian, a New Ager, or a lifelong member of the Green Party. There may come a point when you may question if, in fact, this is your child, instead suspecting that she is the product of an egg dumper, a human cowbird. And someday you may even regret not eating your young.*

The next morning, I had the vice principal, Mr. Whitmore, a large, somber man with the strut of a small-town cop, who has seen it all and heard every excuse, a man who you might suspect has a flask of Wild Turkey stashed in a filing cabinet, haul Rose out of third-year Spanish into his office, where I sat waiting (surprise!). The vice principal frightened me, bringing back the terror of the Chicago public school system where I labored for twelve years with more than one trip to the vice principal for an attitude adjustment. For this visit, I had ironed my best sweatshop Gap pants and a conservative white shirt and put on my least scuffed shoes. I matched up my socks, dug out a tie, and attempted a dimpled Windsor knot. I wanted Mr. Whitmore to see that he was not dealing with trailer trash from the Idaho bomb belt, that we owned bookcases that actually held books, not rifle parts and piles of *TV Guide*, that I did not fear my government, and that even though Rose was failing geometry, this cutting of school was simply an aberration, a slight bump on an otherwise smooth road toward middle-class adulthood. While more tears squeezed down her cheeks, she got a tough-love lecture from an authority figure other than me, a Saturday of detention (with John, unfortunately), and a barrel of public shame.

After glancing at me with a look not unlike the one I received from the young mother at the library, Rose returned to class, and the vice principal turned to me and said, "You know, I'm glad you did that. Most of the parents here try to cover up for their kids. No one takes responsibility anymore. In fact, most parents would not have come in at all."

It was all I could do to smile a thank-you in his direction. What I really wanted to do was rush after Rose, apologize for causing her any discomfort, and then buy her a mint-chip ice cream cone. *(Please don't hate me!)* I felt awful for embarrassing her, like I was headed for an appearance on *The Montel Williams Show*—"Mean Fathers Who Go Too Far and The Daughters Who Hate Them"—but she hasn't cut school since, and she passed geometry.

I LOOK AWAY from the girls across the street to a long staircase leading to the Russell Elementary School playground, where, on a fall day ten years ago, I watched Rose climb those two dozen stairs alone and, with a bag lunch, a cigar box full of colored pens, a gum eraser, and blunt scissors, begin her slow ascent out of my life and into first grade.

I ALWAYS LOOK forward to this after-school hour with Rose. It's an important father-daughter time for us, these twenty-five minutes in the car west over the Idaho-Washington border to Pullman, where we've lived since I remarried. A 1989 Subaru hatchback may be an unlikely setting in which to communicate ethics and values and to reaffirm love and family, but it works for us. Anyway, as a parent of a teenager, you are always off balance—grasping at straws, parenting books, or a bottle of Zoloft. So you tend to stay with any small success. Sociologists love to rattle off statistics about how many minutes per day fathers spend with their children, always discounting the power of silent communication and the value of mere presence, along with the all-important fatherly stare and raised eyebrows. And they rarely speak of how little or erratically a teenager wants to relate with any parent.

Commutes have definite advantages. A moving car does not allow for any getaways; there is only the window to stare out of, although I'm sure we've both felt like flipping the handle, screaming, and jumping out. We know each other so well that we can slash and hurt in the time it takes to tie a shoe. We've taken turns apologizing, yelling, and, in our worse moments, picking at old scabs to get the blood flowing. ("I didn't ask to live in two homes!" is her worst.) But we also discuss our own modest history, the state of affairs with her friends, and sometimes her mom. I let her speak first, and failing that, I ask some questions not so cleverly disguised to elicit more than a yes or a no or a nod, which is hard to see when you are driving fifty-five miles an hour on a two-lane highway. "What did you have for lunch? Did you eat lunch? Where? Do you have any homework?" If it's a good day, a "thumbs-up day," as her first-grade PE teacher called it, she has a lot to say: "I got two poems accepted in the literary magazine, and I think I'm getting an A in chemistry." But if the day's turned sour, and they often do, she gets into the car lugging a stone wall to place between us.

If she is noticeably quiet, I wait it out, knowing that by the time we cross the state line, she might offer something about her lousy day. It might be a friend she's upset with, or a teacher who lost her extra credit, or a substitute teacher who ridiculed her in front of the class about her negative feelings concerning the Vietnam War, or a word in a poem that was changed without her permission. When she lost a homework file to a temperamental school computer, she asked, "Why do we have to be so dependent on these computers?" by which time she was bent over, crying into her hair.

This intersection of the library and school at Jefferson and First Streets is in many ways the core of our fourteen-year history in this town. And although there has been no change in the surroundings of this corner, Rose is now a young woman of seventeen, and somehow I've managed to turn middle-aged, my face a map of well-earned worry wrinkles.

There's comfort with the same surroundings and disruption with too many changes. Lately, as I look past the dignified stone facade of the library, solid and unyielding, to the streets beyond this corner of our world, it's change that has the upper hand. Our little town now rings with the dissonant boom of cul-de-sacs and ugly housing developments with names like Quail Run, Cottage Estates, and Rolling Meadows. We see too many cars on the small streets and a more impatient breed of driver not afraid to lift the middle finger or lean on the horn. On those same crowded roads is more trash from new fast-food joints—a disconcerting stampede of Pizza Huts,

McDonalds, KFCs, Burger Kings, Taco Bells, and Chevron stations with thirty gas pumps. More sameness. Less respect.

I wonder if Rose and her generation feel as much grief as I do with these changes. I can't assume they do, although they have plenty of anxious feelings. It's a common mistake to think our kids are carbon copies of us, that through some kind of experiential osmosis, their lives mirror ours. But Rose is part of a new generation of Westerners who have, in fact, only lived here, while many of us grew up elsewhere. They may have no sense of grief about a wheat field turning into a Wal-Mart. Or a clear-cut in the wilderness. Or a new trailer park on the edge of town that replaced an aspen grove. Do we appear angry and sad to our children when they listen to us discuss environmental and social issues? Are we supposed to teach them that grief? Have we already?

I think back to an assignment I gave Spokane high school students when I was invited there as a guest writer: "What are you afraid of?"

Making a mistake. Rapists. Going to college. Becoming my father. Staying the same too long. The environment becoming bad. The future. Death of a loved one. Admitting my love for another. Spiders. My grandmother's perfume. Losing my convictions. Loneliness. Leaving behind what I love. Prejudice. Being torn from all I believe in. Not being able to make a difference. Machines. Dark basements. Raising my children wrong.

We should memorize this list.

I KNOW SOME THINGS about my daughter. My life is defined by being her father. Rose affects me at both a cellular and an emotional level, in ways so subtle, deep, and even biological that I cannot imagine ever living in a world in which she did not exist. She is always on my mind, sometimes out front, sometimes at the edges, but always there. (Thus the worry wrinkles and crow's-feet.) Yet, I cannot always remember her early years with much detail. We did not keep a baby book. There are no videos, thank goodness. Relatives were all back in the Midwest or the East, not a part of my life then. Photos were few, and now they are scattered between two households. I mostly remember being tired and frustrated, trying to climb out of poverty and sort out why I wasn't becoming middle-class like everyone else in my generation. For several years, I made $130 a week, and each time my boss would hand me the check, he would hold the other end for just a second too long and ask, "Do you mind waiting a day before you cash this?"

Despite my erratic memory, there are times, seasonal and aromatic in nature, involving light or sounds or colors, when I do remember details. The way she felt on my back as I carried her down the street. How she would point and crow when I would tell her new words to add to her growing vocabulary. The way she would greet me when I returned at the end of the day, exhausted from picking daffodils, driving grain trucks, or cooking omelets.

Rose is leaving, not permanently, but certainly she's ascending another flight of stairs to a new level of life, and this time the lump in my throat is the size of a pineapple. The question is not whether she is prepared, but whether I am.

I never imagined how fast we would arrive at this crossroads. Rose is at that magical age, on the doorstep of possibility, about to enter a rarefied state of young adulthood where excitement and enchantment collide, and the world is vast and beckoning. I am mostly settled, feeling those enhanced emotional moments of inspiration less and less but instead experiencing a richness that I never felt at seventeen, a context and texture that comes with being alive for four decades. Some goals remain. I still hope to walk the Pacific Crest Trail, or visit Tuscany, or learn to play tenor saxophone, get a degree in natural science, play guitar like Chet Atkins, and get published in the *New Yorker*.

Rose bounces up to the car with Rachel in tow. They have a plan that involves volleyball and bikes, and can we get a snack on the way home? If I could preserve this moment, bottle it and place it in a locked chest, I would. *This is my life,* I say to myself. *Everything I could ever want is right in front of me.* The girls get in the car and we're off, the three of us a perfect picture of energy and gossip and glorious laughter.

A FEW WEEKS LATER, on Father's Day, I decide we should drive to Elk River, a sleepy timber town on life support. Not long ago, customers at the Elk Butte Log Inn watched a logging truck rumble by every three minutes. Those days are mostly over—in the immediate area, at least. The population sign says 149. Another sign in an abandoned building says COMING SOON, but no one believes it. The only school finally closed several years ago, after graduating its last two high school students, and has been replaced with a few gift shops. Just outside of town, we are delayed by hundreds of cattle sauntering down the middle of the highway. At the end of the herd is a family on foot using sticks and tree limbs to keep the cattle on track.

Some arm-twisting was involved to get Rose to agree to this trip. "Can't I just take you out for breakfast?" she asked, looking pained. We reached a deal. I told her we didn't have to leave until eleven, and I agreed to buy her a steamed milk on the way.

We rent a canoe at Huckleberry Heaven and put in near the Elk River pond. First we have to negotiate a narrow channel. We have only canoed together one other time, and it's a struggle to synchronize our J strokes. We crash into a few bushes along the bank, get stuck on every sandbar, and manage to cover a hundred yards going sideways. Neither of us gets mad, and the idea of Rose being in a canoe under paternal duress passes with each paddle. Besides, we are out on the water with the turtles, a family of Canada geese, ducks, and a watchful pair of osprey. I don't ever want the day to end.

As we eat cold pasta salad and rhubarb muffins in silence (while high-centered on a sandbar), I wonder what Rose is afraid of, but I don't ask. She has enough to think about. Instead I say, "There's some potato salad and grapes if you're still hungry." I think I'm finally beginning to get it: Rose is mostly grown-up. I need to step back even more and let her grow into her life. And I need to get on with mine.

After two hours of canoeing, the last part of which is spent floating in circles around a smaller pond full of warm algae that I tell Rose is actually body-snatcher people, we pull the canoe out on the bank and head back. "Let's take the long way, the dirt road to Helmer. We haven't been on it in a few years," I suggest, wanting to draw the afternoon out into twilight and to go somewhere that hasn't been subdivided. But even out here, there is change.

After just a mile of driving comes evidence of every conceivable type of logging practice: clear-cuts, selected cuts, burns, and new plantings. New roads are everywhere, with numbered signs, and many have the ubiquitous locked green gates. Rusty culverts lie in piles like intestines, along with discarded steel cables, parked bulldozers, and other earth movers. I look for a campground that I'm convinced is out here, but I can't find it among all the chaos. Signs warn us to watch for heavy equipment, but it's Sunday, and even the work of destruction needs to rest.

I start in with my usual rant and rave about all the new roads, the wreck and ruin, the shrinking habitat for animals, overpopulation, and de-evolution, but after a few minutes, I shut up. I can tell where this is going. What do I expect Rose to do? Come out here and blockade a bulldozer? Spike a tree? She's heard all this before. She'll figure it out for herself if she hasn't already. Or maybe she won't. These are my struggles. She has the rest of her life to acquire her own.

Instead of delivering a meaningless lecture, I pull over at the crest of the hill, and we sit for a moment as the sun fades to look at what is still there: dark cedar forests and wide, wet meadows of tall grass, skunk cabbage, and wild flowers; creeks that make you weep with their simplicity. Then I start the Subaru up and we drive home, taking our time, following the back roads just like all the times before. Just like nothing has changed or ever will.

Sons

Anna Viadero

SONS ENTER MY HEART at two-year intervals. At opposite ends of the year. One under a night sky filled with diamonds. One into a day gone gray with fog. Their lungs as strong as bellows. Their cries in the beginning foreign to me. Now, years later, they are sounds I remember the way a master ornithologist remembers birds' songs.

Sons enter my heart. The first one longer than my arm. His knees knit as he grew inside me, and his tendons shortened so that his legs came out bent and stiff and crooked as that old man in the nursery rhyme. I pulled his legs like taffy, pulled to make him straight and perfect and whole so that he would become as tall as his great-grandfather's brother, the Russian guard.

The second one born screaming—his head covered with the deep red hair of long-dead ancestors so that I must count backward into our histories, as on a number line, and run deep into negative numbers before I find Incarnation's mother's sister back in Santander, Spain. Her hot Latin blood runs through this son, who parries with my heart like a fencer, prancing up to threaten me, then backing away. Over time, I drown myself in my own pity trying to decode him. I walk into the ocean of my frustration with rocks in my pockets, his cries at my back like a foghorn calling out to me from shore.

Sons enter my heart with lentils and pea pods from their garden. The scent of soil in one dirty kiss. The slime of red efts in the webs of their fingers. Their innocence as potent as opium. I breathe it in until I almost break, then just one sniff more.

Sons enter my heart those nights when ghosts appear on the floor all around my youngest's bed. They bob there in his dreams, released from the ocean of nightmares his tiny bed navigates nightly. In escaping, he says, he steps on their heads like rocks in a stream and passes to the safety of the shore that I am sleeping on, dreaming of a sunny beach in Cuba, *café con leche,* my husband whose hands melt me like butter. This son enters my bed, enters the crook of my left arm, head to my chest, to hear my heartsong, the way bandits set one ear to the rails to see if a train is on the way and when they know it is, they move to ambush it the way this son ambushes me—completely.

My sons go from smooth to hairy in a season. Grow a head taller than me. Push away and run circles around me that grow more and more distant. First it was around the pine tree in our yard, then a quarter mile down the road to the brook. Now it's to Florida with a sports team or to Paris with classmates.

My sons go from speaking my language to speaking in tongues overnight. They received their holy spirit, are baptized into their own generation, washed over with words and songs downloaded from the Internet. Return to me only when they're feverish or vomiting. Look completely perplexed when their father tells them to thank me.

"What for?" they ask, not really knowing or believing there's a need. Feeling, I imagine, that thanking me would be like thanking the sun for rising or their hearts for beating or the ground for splitting each spring to spit out tulips.

Sons enter my heart on the coattails of destiny, with their father's jaw and their uncle's frame. They are my heroes; they pave paths through the vacant lot of my soul, awakening pieces of me I had set aside. My sons enter my heart, climb deep inside me, jiggle all the stagnant parts of me, and exclaim like Einstein, "We can get these working!" They connect wires from yesterday to tomorrow and shock me into existence, turn me over like an old engine, and when I turn to thank them, they say, "What for?" not knowing or believing how dead my battery was after carrying the sorrows of Eastern Europe all these years—my immigrant parents' insecurities, my four sisters who gyroscoped around me like starved cats.

Sons enter my heart and nest there as a colicky infant whose cries made my heart crumble, as an impetuous two-year-old who ran too fast down hills and came up with scabbed lips, as a fifth-grader who kept one lumpy thumb nestled in his soft-tongued mouth, as a too-young fourth-grader put in to pitch with two men out and bases loaded and he pulled out the win as easily as a magician pulls a rabbit out of a hat! As a six-foot-tall teen just accepted to the college of his choice who holds me, his proud and sobbing mother, to his chest the way I held him for the first time eighteen years ago under that night sky filled with diamonds. I smiled as widely then as he is now, feeling very much the same as he is—like I hit the lottery big-time. His little brother the athlete steps in and thumps my back three times to quiet me.

Sons enter my heart and set up permanent dwellings, dig cellar holes, build houses that are meant to last with firm timbers, set them together with perfect, hand-hewn pegs. They leave the lights on for me now when they go out so I remember they'll be home again soon.

Freshman Orientation

Alex Witchel

BY THE TIME he left we still weren't ready, which makes no sense at all. You spend four years of angst with a kid who's trying to get into college, and once he does, what are you supposed to do, tell him to stay home?

My husband, Frank, and I figured that once Simon, my younger stepson, actually left, we'd muddle through, somehow. After all, we had taken his older brother, Nathaniel, to college four years ago and survived. But the tiny detail we had conveniently forgotten was that Simon was home that entire time. Our lives still revolved neatly around midterms and finals and track practice, as safe and sound as when we were kids ourselves.

Then suddenly—or so it seemed—we were growing up. Or at least Simon was. And while it was safe to assume that he also had mixed feelings about leaving, the tribal language of grunts favored by teenage boys prevailed. What had been a lifetime conversation about every conceivable topic became a series of uh-huhs and

I–don't–knows, sometimes punctuated by a slightly apologetic smile. As topics went, that tired and sorry cliché of an empty nest had become too sharp and fresh for dissection.

But by mid-August, when his friends' exodus began, I thought the moment for our sit-down had come. Hah! Every time he showed up for dinner, he brought company—a friend, his girl-friend—guaranteeing a talk-free zone. You can't very well burst into tears in front of a girlfriend who's just been doing the same thing.

Finally, I did manage to ask when he wanted to pack up his clothes. He looked at me blankly. Now, Simon has been shuttling between two homes since before he turned three. I imagined he would be feeling tremendous relief to finally land in one bed, one room, where the chances of locating a social studies textbook would increase ten-fold. But he didn't answer—he left me talking with his very sweet girlfriend while he disappeared. Later, Frank told me that he had asked Simon the same question, but that he wouldn't pack a thing.

"I want to keep my clothes here," he had said, and Frank and I were genuinely touched that his connection to our home was so strong that he didn't want anything as trivial as college to get in its way. The only problem was, he was still going.

In the week before he left, neither Frank nor I slept through the night. I would stay awake for two hours, then fall asleep as he awoke for the next shift. I imagined that we had both gone back in time to when we were first married, and we were once again waiting for the knock. Our wedding took place four days after Simon turned seven. Before we moved, he had spent nights in his dad's "bachelor" apartment, sleeping next to him in his bed. Somehow, the brand new beds we had bought for the specially designated "kids' room" in the new apartment didn't have the same allure. So the knock started, that small yet determined sound.

"I can't sleep," Simon would announce, and Frank would scoop him up into the bed, holding him close until he drifted off. Eventually, Frank would carry him back to his own bed, where he would wake up the next morning, completely cheerful. But for those first few months, the knock came again and again, until one day, just like that, it stopped. He seemed to finally understand that no matter what else had changed, his daddy was going to let him in—every time. But no matter how hard we tried to will ourselves backward to that distant instant when we were in charge of making things better, the calendar beat us.

The night before the dorms opened, we all assembled for dinner: Simon and Nathaniel, their mom, Frank, and I. Simon had his "last" steak, before his meal plan kicked in, and eager to get on with his life as a college student, had made plans to meet a friend. The group of us walked him there, and as the rest went ahead, I hooked my arm through Simon's and pulled him close.

"What's going on with you?" I asked. "Every time I've seen you these last few weeks, you've made sure someone is there so we can't have a real conversation." Though he had spoken with his dad alone, he had still skirted the issue of departure.

He stopped, under the glare of a street light, and looked at me, hard. "You know," he said, "there's just so much of this separation stuff you can do." I looked at him, hard, thinking about the relationship I have made with him and his brother. I am now the kind of person I had wished for when I was growing up: the adult who loves them full time and completely voluntarily—genetic obligation not included. I chose them, and they chose me back. Our bond endures with less of the drama, the static, of the other. I had to honor that.

I smiled the wry smile he was waiting to see and unhooked my arm from his. "I get it," I said, as his friend walked into view. "I do."

The next day, the move went quickly. Simon's dorm room was only one flight up, and he had indeed packed lightly. As his mom hung his clothes in the closet, I folded the rest into his dresser and his father and brother made his bed. Then the three adults went to the meeting for freshman parents, where we were encouraged to be saner than the "bad examples"—like the couple who actually bought a condo next to the campus. I laughed along with everyone else and wondered why that was such a terrible idea.

Afterward, we walked back to Simon's room. In the hour in which we were gone, a CD player had been plugged in, and music blared from behind closed doors. Simon was with his two room-mates, talking and laughing, right at home—his home. With our chores now done, we had somehow become guests. Simon hugged us each in turn, and we were all very brave, and by the time Frank and I went to sleep that night, we had two grown children, not one.

So far, the email messages have been good. He sounds happy on the phone. In our buoyant moments, we imagine where he is and what he's doing and how much fun he's having. But there are other moments, too, when his father is bereft, and I wrap my arms around him—and I don't take them away—and I tell him not to be sad. He's coming home again, he really is. After all, his pants are here.

Alfalfa

Hal Ackerman

Her room smells of alfalfa even though she has taken the rabbits.
The stages of her life have settled into an archaeology of smells.
The sweet dander of guinea pigs. Sour turtle bowls.
Saddles redolent of horse piss and her own gamey adolescence.
Weed. Incense.
Her first boy. Her second boy.
When a friend lied about her at school and everyone believed it.
When she did not make ballet.

I would rather think of alfalfa. Of her uncle's farm in Kentucky.
Her small hand on the wheel of the tractor.
Looking with intent across the unplowed field.
Her hair white as corn silk. Her voice all made of music.
Her spirit an unhunted bird,
Gathering bits of shiny colored things it saw that it liked.

I don't want to think of the empty bed frame
Waiting for the moving boys to dismantle.
The mattress is already gone.
Gone with Ani DiFranco and the 3AM phone calls.
And everything that was nailed or taped to the walls.
She has left behind the dresser that she built herself, refusing help.
It wobbles like an ancient parent you have to help to the bathroom.
The wrong size screws protrude from the knobs.
The drawers are emptied chrysalises splayed open like the
     tongues of exhausted oxen.

She calls to give me her new phone number.
I write it down, thinking it is something I should already know.
Something I should be teaching her. She will know things first now.
If she gets cancer, it is she who will break the news to me.
I tell her that without her instructive derision I go into the world
     unfit for public display. Hair unkempt. Wearing unmatched socks.
Tufts of spiny filament sprouting from my earlobes.
I threaten to wear slippers and a tattered robe to the supermarket.
But she is unmoved by pity to return.
So I describe the cream of cauliflower soup I have made for dinner.
The clever substitutions of ingredients to keep it nondairy.
The dressing for the artichokes and the roasted yams.
Dad, she says, I don't live there anymore.
Ah, I say.
And now it is she who fills the silence:
"Don't you want me to live in the world and be self-sufficient?

Isn't that what this whole childhood nonsense was all about?"
No, I argue, after a certain point I am opposed to metamorphsis.

But even that is not true.
I tell her yes. Yes to everything. Yes and yes.
And of course yes.
Only just.
You know,
not yet.

Flown Away, Left Behind

Anna Quindlen

I WAS SOMETHING of an accidental mother. I don't mean that in the old traditional whoops! way; it's just that while I barreled through my twenties convinced that having a baby would be like carrying a really large and inconvenient tote bag that I could never put down, I awoke one day at thirty and, in what now seems an astonishingly glib leap of faith, decided I wanted that tote bag in the very worst way. It was as though my ovaries had taken possession of my brain. Less than a year later an infant had taken possession of everything else. My brain no longer worked terribly well, especially when I added to that baby another less than two years later, and a third fairly soon after that.

That was twenty years ago. You do the math. The first one went to China to polish his Mandarin. The second left for college in the fall. I still have a chick in the nest, and what a chick she is, but increasingly it feels like an aerie too large for its occupants. Recently I told her we were going to be doing something we had always done as a family. "We don't have that family anymore," she said. (Here I pause to remove the shiv from between my ribs, breathe deeply and smile.)

Tell me at your peril that the flight of my kids into successful adulthood is hugely liberating, that I will not believe how many hours are in the day, that my husband and I can see the world, that I can throw myself into my job. My world is in this house, and I already had a great job into which I'd thrown myself for two decades. No, not the writing job—the motherhood job. I was good at it, if I do say so myself, and because I was, I've now been demoted to part-time work. Soon I will attain emerita status. This stinks.

I wonder if this has a particular edge for the women of my generation, who found themselves pursuing mothering in a new sort of way. We professionalized it, and in doing so made ourselves a tiny bit ridiculous and more than a little crazy. Women who left their children in the care of others to work for pay often wound up, by necessity and habit, scheduling their mother life as they did their working one. (See us logging teacher conferences into our PDAs in the parking lot of the preschool.) Women who eschewed the job market despite the gains of women within it sometimes wound up making motherhood into a surrogate work world, full of school meetings and endless athletic teams. (See us chairing bake sales even though it would be cheaper to write a check than to make brownies.) For both groups, the unexamined child was not worth having: from late crawling to bad handwriting to mediocre SATs, all was grist for the worry mill. Motherhood changed from a role into a calling. Our poor kids.

The end result is that the empty nest is emptier than ever before; after all, at its center was a role, a vocation, a nameless something so enormous that a good deal had to be sacrificed for it, whether sleep or self or money or ambition or peace of mind. Those sacrifices— or accommodations, for those of us waxing poetic about their end—became the warp and woof of our lives; first we got used to them and then before we knew it they had become obsolete. Those of you waiting for your babies to sleep through the night will be amazed how quickly they come to sleep through the afternoon after a night out.

For years I wrote only between the hours of nine and three, when the children were at school. (God forbid they should actually see me work.) Now that two of the children live at school and one has play rehearsal, basketball games and random hanging-out when school is done, I still write only between the hours of nine and three. It has become my routine; I did not choose to change it. In the kitchen is a magnet that says MOM IS NOT MY REAL NAME. See our heads snap up in the supermarket when someone yells the word, as surely as our milk once let down when we heard a baby, any baby, cry.

Much has been written about the pernicious nature of having it all, the perfection syndrome required of women who must play so many roles in the lives of others, jamming loving obligations into days that feel too short, discussing endlessly how to balance work and home. But many of us eventually ratcheted up our metabolisms accordingly. First overfull was a cross, then a challenge, eventually a commonplace. Anything less is empty.

It's not simply the loss of these particular people, living here day in, day out, the bickering, the inside jokes, the cereal bowls in the sink and the towels in the hamper—all right, on the floor. It was who I was with them: the general to their battalion, the president to their cabinet. The Harpo to their Groucho, Zeppo and Chico. Sometimes I go into their rooms and just stand, touching their books, looking out their windows. "The shrine," the youngest says derisively, although she misses the other two as much as I do. But she has her own plans, has one eye now on the glitter past the window glass. At the end of the month she heads Down Under on a six-week school exchange, leaving the bulletin board, the photograph albums and the wallpaper with butterflies on it behind. And me, of course. Three rooms empty, full of the ghosts of my very best self. Mom is my real name. It is, it is.

About the Contributors

Hal Ackerman has been on the UCLA screenwriting faculty for twenty years. His book *Write Screenplays That Sell: The Ackerman Way* renders all previous intellectual thought on the subject obsolete. His one-man play, *Blue Sundays: How Prostate Cancer Made a Man out of Me,* opens in Los Angeles in spring 2005.

Stevan Allred's fiction and journalism have appeared in many publications, including *Beloit Fiction Journal, Lite: Baltimore's Literary Newspaper, Rosebud, Berkeley Fiction Review, Portland Mercury, Stepfamily Advocate,* and others. He was awarded an Oregon Literary Fellowship in 2004. He lives outside of Estacada, Oregon, with his wife and two sons. He's wondering if it's any easier when the second child gets a tattoo.

Peter Applebome writes the "Our Town" column for *The New York Times* and is the author of *Scout's Honor: A Father's Unlikely Foray into the Woods* and *Dixie Rising: How the South Is Shaping American Values, Politics, and Culture.* He lives in Chappaqua, New York, with his wife, Mary Catherine Bounds, and two children, Ben and Emma. Despite three years of Scouting, he still can't tie his knots.

Dave Barry is a writer whose humor column for *The Miami Herald* appeared in more than five hundred newspapers in the United States and abroad for twenty years. In 1988, he won the Pulitzer Prize for commentary. Many people are still trying to figure out how this happened. Barry has also written a total of twenty-five books, including *Dave Barry's Greatest Hits, Dave Barry's Complete Guide to Guys*, and *Dave Barry Turns 50*. Barry lives in Miami, Florida, with his wife, Michelle, a sportswriter. He has a son, Rob, and a daughter, Sophie, neither of whom thinks he's funny.

Nancy Blakey is a freelance writer, parent educator, and author of the *Mudpies Activity Book* series. Her latest book is *Go Outside!*. She and her husband raised a daughter and three sons and survived the teen years with luck, a sense of humor, and family work summers in Alaska. She can be reached at nancyblakey.com.

Rebecca Boucher lives in Brooklyn with her husband and their four children. Her work has appeared in several publications and in the anthology *Toddler: Real-Life Stories of Those Fickle, Irrational, Urgent, Tiny People We Love*.

W. Bruce Cameron was voted America's number-one humor columnist by the National Society of Newspaper Columnists in 2003. His book, *8 Simple Rules for Dating My Teenage Daughter*, became a *New York Times* bestseller and was the basis for the ABC television show *8 Simple Rules*. Having written a book on getting along with teenage girls, which is impossible, Mr. Cameron then turned his attention to another impossible feat, changing men and their habits, in *How to Remodel a Man*. He lives in Los Angeles and has three children.

David Carkeet has written several novels, most recently *The Error of Our Ways*. His new memoir, *Campus Sexpot*, won the Creative Nonfiction Award given by the Association of Writers and Writing Programs, and will be published in September 2005 by the University of Georgia Press. For many years he taught linguistics and writing at the University of Missouri–St. Louis. The father of three honest daughters—Anne, Laurie, and Molly—he now lives in Middlesex, Vermont.

Roz Chast sold her first cartoon to *The New Yorker* in 1978, and her work has appeared regularly in its pages ever since. Her cartoons have also appeared in such diverse publications as *Scientific American* and *Redbook*. Her latest book is *The Party After You Left: Collected Cartoons 1995–2003*.

Connie E. Curry is a nonfiction humor writer from Ohio whose three children and granddaughter are her tools for putting laughter into words. She won the annual Thurber Treat Humor Writing Contest in 2001. Her work has been published in *Country Living*, *Reunions Magazine*, *Women with Wheels*, and *Shotgun Sports*. Curry is a humor columnist for *South West Sentinel*, a newspaper in Georgia, and she is a member of the Write Life Writing Group, the Delaware Writing Group, and Ohio Writer.

Louise Erdrich is a Native American novelist, poet, short-story writer, and essayist. She is the author of two volumes of poetry and several best-selling and award-winning novels, including *Love Medicine*,

The Beet Queen, Tracks, The Master Butchers Singing Club, and *Four Souls.* Her memoir of motherhood, *The Blue Jay's Dance,* was her first non-fiction work. She lives in Minnesota with her children, who help her run a small independent bookstore called The Birchbark.

Flor Fernandez Barrios was born in Cuba and immigrated to the United States in 1970 when she was fourteen, an experience she recounts in her memoir, *Blessed by Thunder: Memoir of a Cuban Girlhood.* Her writings have been anthologized in several collections, including *Storming Heaven's Gate: An Anthology of Spiritual Writings by Women.* She is a psychotherapist and nationally known workshop leader on multicultural issues and spirituality. She recently completed her second book, *The Mask of Oya,* a collection of stories about her work.

Nina Gaby resides in central Vermont, where she parents not only an adolescent but also a husband, a slew of pets, and a thirteen-room inn. A former therapist and award-winning ceramic artist, she has been published in several anthologies and was recently awarded a fellowship to Vermont Studio Center, where she will be exploring mixed-media visual art with contemporary literary themes. She is at work on a book tentatively titled "Therapy, Stewardship, Running an Inn, and What a Girl Won't Do to Get Out of Wearing Stockings to Work."

Daniel Glick's most recent book is *Monkey Dancing: A Father, Two Kids, and a Journey to the Ends of the Earth,* which won a Colorado

Book Award in 2004. A former news correspondent for *Newsweek* for many years, Glick has written for numerous publications, including *National Geographic, Harper's, Rolling Stone, The New York Times Magazine, The Washington Post Magazine, Outside, Esquire, Men's Journal, Sports Afield, National Wildlife,* and *Wilderness.* He lives in Colorado with his son and daughter.

Debra Gwartney is a writer, editor, instructor, and mother of four daughters. Her memoir pieces, essays, and fiction have appeared in a wide array of publications, including *Salon, Creative Nonfiction, Fourth Genre, The Kenyon Review, Washington Square Review,* and *The Oregonian.* She lives in Eugene, Oregon.

Susan Hodara is a freelance journalist who contributes regularly to *The New York Times* and whose work has appeared in *Communication Arts, Salon, Parents,* a *Showtime* website, and numerous other publications. She serves as consulting editor for Family Communications, which publishes four New York–area monthly parenting newspapers. As editor in chief of Manhattan-based *Big Apple Parent,* she received a Best Editorial award from Parenting Publications of America for her monthly column. She lives with her husband and two teenage daughters in Westchester County, New York.

Irene Hopkins lives in Seattle with her husband and two teenage daughters. She writes a newsletter for the University of Washington Medical Center and runs the Beauty and Cancer Program, an appearance support program for oncology patients. She is at work on a memoir about her family's experiences boating through the coastal waters of the Pacific Northwest.

Gail Hudson's personal essays about family relationships have appeared in numerous publications, including *Child, Parents, Utne,* and *Self.* As contributing editor for *Child* magazine she wrote a book on conflict resolution, *Child Magazine's Guide to Quarreling.* She resides in Seattle with her husband and two teenage children.

Roberta Israeloff is an essayist, short-story writer, and author of several books, most recently *Kindling the Flame: Reflections on Ritual, Faith, and Family.* Currently at work on a novel, she lives and teaches writing in East Northport, New York.

Barbara Kingsolver is the best-selling author of numerous works of fiction and nonfiction, most recently the collection of essays titled *Small Wonder.* Her novels include *The Poisonwood Bible, The Bean Trees, Animal Dreams, Pigs in Heaven,* and *Prodigal Summer.* She is also the author of a collection of poetry, *Another America.* She was awarded the National Humanities Medal in 2000. After many years of living in Tucson, Arizona, Kingsolver now resides in southern Appalachia with her family.

Stephen J. Lyons is the author of *Landscape of the Heart: Writings on Daughters and Journeys,* a single father's memoir, and *A View from the Inland Northwest: Everyday Life in America.* His articles, essays, and reviews have been published in various national magazines and newspapers, including *The Washington Post, Salon, USA Today, Newsweek, Chicago Sun-Times, Sierra, San Francisco Chronicle, The Sun,* and many others. A native of the South Side of Chicago who lived for thirty years in the West, Lyons now resides in a small farming town in central Illinois.

Joyce Maynard, a longtime journalist and former *New York Times* columnist, is the author of the best-selling memoir *At Home in the World* and six novels, including *To Die For* and *The Cloud Charmer,* a young adult book to be published in June 2005. Maynard wrote *Parenting* magazine's column "A Mother's Days" for many years, as well as the nationally syndicated column "Domestic Affairs." The mother of three grown children, she makes her home in Northern California. She can be reached through her website, www.joycemaynard.com.

Elizabeth Nunez is a City University of New York Distinguished Professor at Medgar Evers College and the author of five novels: *Grace, Discretion, Bruised Hibiscus, Beyond the Limbo Silence,* and *When Rocks Dance.* She lives outside of New York City.

Laura Smith Porter writes a weekly column on family life called "Dispatches from the Home Front" for the *Worcester Telegram & Gazette.* Her essays and fiction have been published in magazines, newspapers, and literary anthologies, including *FamilyFun, The Philosophical Mother, The Boston Parents' Paper,* and *Three-Ring Circus: How Real Couples Balance Marriage, Work, and Family.* She and her husband have finally learned to fit all of the pieces of their teenage son's drum set in the car.

Anna Quindlen is the best-selling author of four novels, *Blessings, Black and Blue, One True Thing*, and *Object Lessons*, and several non-fiction books, including *Loud and Clear, A Short Guide to a Happy Life, Living Out Loud, Thinking Out Loud,* and *How Reading Changed My Life*. She has also written two children's books, *The Tree That Came to Stay* and *Happily Ever After*. Her *New York Times* column, "Public and Private," won a Pulitzer Prize in 1992. Her column now appears every other week in *Newsweek*.

Linda Rue Quinn lives with her husband, Bryan, and two teen-agers, Paul and Cindy, in Chester, South Carolina. She is a member of the South Carolina Writers Workshop. She writes because it is cheaper than therapy.

Helen Klein Ross lives in Manhattan with her husband and two teenage daughters. Her writing has appeared in *Mid-American Review, Quick Fiction,* and *Mothering,* and has received honorable mention in *The Atlantic Monthly* and *Glimmer Train Stories*. She has been nominated for a Pushcart Prize in 2005 and is at work on a novel and a collection of poems about mothering.

Anna Viadero, a first-generation American, is a writer living in Montague, Massachusetts. Her essays about her own family and her family of origin have been published in many anthologies. She is a frequent commentator on public radio in New England.

Jeffrey K. Wallace is currently teaching creative writing at Chapman University in Orange, California, and at the Orange County High School of the Arts in its Creative Writing Conservatory. His essays have appeared in *Los Angeles Times*, *The Orange County Register*, and *Family Circle* magazine. He is a happily married, rapidly aging father of two.

Marion Winik is a commentator for National Public Radio's *All Things Considered* and the author of several works of nonfiction, including *Telling, First Comes Love, The Lunch-Box Chronicles*, and *Above Us Only Sky*, forthcoming from Seal Press in October 2005. She lives in Glen Rock, Pennsylvania, with her husband, writer Crispin Sartwell, and their many children.

Alex Witchel is a staff writer at *The New York Times Magazine*. She is the author of *Girls Only: Sleepovers, Squabbles, Tuna Fish and Other Facts of Family Life,* based on columns she wrote for *The New York Times,* and the novel *Me Times Three*, which was a national bestseller.

Credits and Copyright Notices

Acknowledgments

THE WRITING OF A BOOK has sometimes been compared, by women writers at least, to the birthing of a child—long and often tedious months culminating in the arduous but exhilarating act of creation. This book has taken somewhat longer than nine months to produce, so we'll liken it instead to the experience of raising a child: Both require perspective and balance, an appreciation for the power of laughter, and a willingness to hang in there, even when you would rather lie down and nap. And yes, it takes a village, in the form of loving and supportive family members, steady and patient friends, and the collective wisdom of a larger community—parents, grandparents, educators, mentors. Our book would not exist without such help, and for that we are most grateful.

First and foremost, we would like to thank the hundreds of writers who responded to our call for submissions to this collection. We were amazed and gratified by the care and passion each writer brought to the ongoing conversation about raising our teenagers. It was with great regret that we had to limit the book to a select number of essays.

We are enormously grateful to our contributors, whose brilliant writing and parenting wisdom touched our hearts and minds. They were an inspiration to us, and it was a privilege to work with each one. We thank them for the opportunity to share their words with a wider audience.

We would especially like to express our gratitude to our Seal Press editor, Ingrid Emerick, whose insightful and sensitive reading helped us at every turn and whose encouragement always propelled us forward. This book improved greatly under her guidance. We thank her for her excellent editing talents and wonderful friendship.

Many thanks are due to the capable and hardworking team at Avalon Publishing Group, including our managing editor, Marisa Solís, our copyeditor, Laura Mazer, and our publicist, Krista Rafanello.

We'd also like to thank Elizabeth Wales, whose early conversations about this book helped to shape our ideas and steer us in the right direction. We are grateful for her assistance.

We would have never made it through our years of parenting, much less this book project, without our friends and family, who have offered support, advice, and camaraderie. No amount of thanks is enough. Our space is too limited to name each person who has helped us along the way, but we would especially like to thank the following:

F.C.:

I'd like to thank my parents, Edythe Conlon and the late Andrew Conlon, for their love and encouragement throughout my life. Parental advice is often half-heeded, if listened to at all. It was not until I became a parent that I began to truly appreciate the wisdom of my own upbringing.

To my sister (help-line extraordinaire), brothers, and siblings-in-law on both sides of the family, thanks for the great company and for providing terrific role models in parenting. Each one of my nieces and nephews could be a poster child for the way we wish our kids to turn out—smart, funny, talented, courteous, and kind. I am lucky to have such a fun-loving tribe to call my own.

I am grateful to have a community of friends who've taught me the many ways to be a parent. For hours of conversation about parenting teenagers and help when it was needed, I thank my dear friend Mary-Carter Creech, the late Deborah Kaufmann (you are sorely missed), and Laura Lilly, friend and confidant all these long years—from mischief in our seventh-grade homeroom to rock concerts, road trips, and beyond.

Before I ever learned to rock a baby to sleep, I was neck-deep in the world of Nintendo, Little League games, and handmade beaded earrings. That is because I became a stepmom before I was a mom, when my stepdaughter was twelve and my stepson was eight. Erin and Scott McKittrick opened their hearts—even the doors to their rooms—and welcomed me in, and for that I am profoundly grateful. I learned some important lessons from them about the integrity and intelligence of teenagers (okay, and some clever ways to fabricate one's whereabouts on a Saturday night), which I hope to remember when their little brother hits seventh grade next year. My everlasting thanks to them both.

To my son Connor, who lights up my world, a million thanks for putting up with my hours spent in front of the computer, tap tap tapping, and on the phone, talk talk talking. I think he is more pleased than anyone to see this book reach completion. I am thankful every day for his happy presence in my life.

Finally, to my husband, John McKittrick, whose infinite patience has been a wonder to behold, my gratitude and love. My life as a parent would be far less fun without his steady hand. His support has been crucial during this project, from giving me a needed dad's perspective on the book to cheerfully ignoring the precipitous decline in my housekeeping standards. I owe him a world of thanks.

G.H.:

A special nod goes to my parents, James and Patricia Hudson. As the youngest child and designated rebel, I gave them hell when I hit adolescence. To this day, my teen years are the stuff of family legends. Thank you for putting up with me and only smirking occasionally when my own children hit adolescence.

Many thanks to my brother, Jim, and sister, Judy, and their spouses, Margo and Matt. They took on the parenting role years before I did. Seeing the joy and devotion they brought to parenthood as well as the amazing children they brought forth gave me the courage to become a mother.

I couldn't do it without my mothering support group. To Lynn Fleming, my partner in crime throughout adolescence, thank you for all the years of loyal friendship and for being my daughter's fairy godmother. Crème de menthe and *Abbey Road* forever. Many thanks to Robin Rothenberg for godmothering my son and always reminding me that I was woman before I became a mom. A big hug to Trish Maharam: Thank you for being my special confidant, ideal writing companion, and "other mother" to Gabrielle. To Dianne Grob, many thanks for always helping me see more clearly and laugh more often. My friend Laurie Riepe entered motherhood on the same day, at the same hospital, with the same midwife as me. Thank you, Laurie, for your commitment to truth in any conversation and for inviting me to be Jackson's godmother, one of the best gifts I've ever received. My writing colleagues Jordan Buck, Connie Feutz, and Brenda Peterson deserve a special thanks for all their loving support and guidance.

To my husband, Hal Abbott, thank you for being a great partner in parenting and a great partner in marriage. I am grateful to have found both in one man. To my daughter, Gabrielle, at age eighteen, thank you for all the ways you challenged and delighted me during your teen years. You have been my inspiration for this book. To my son, Tennessee, at age thirteen, the benefit of being the second child is that I'll be more relaxed this time around, but the downside is that I'll also be a lot more savvy. I am truly excited to see how your teen years unfold. I love you both so much. It is an honor to be your mother.

About the Editors

Faith Conlon was the publisher of Seal Press for two decades and is now a freelance editor. She is the coeditor of several books, including *A Woman Alone: Travel Tales from Around the Globe, Gifts of the Wild: A Woman's Book of Adventure,* and *The Things That Divide Us.* She lives in Seattle with her husband and son.

Gail Hudson is an author, essayist, editor, and creative writing teacher. Her personal essays have appeared in numerous publications, including *Child, Parents, Utne, Self,* and *Body & Soul.* She reviews books for many publishing-industry publications, including *Publishers Weekly,* and for Amazon.com. She lives in Seattle with her husband and two children.

Selected Titles from Seal Press

For more than twenty-five years, Seal Press has published groundbreaking books. By women. For women. Visit our website at www.sealpress.com.

Beyond One: Growing a Family and Getting a Life by Jennifer Bingham Hull. $14.95, 1-58005-104-9. This wise and humorous book addresses the concerns of parents who are making the leap from one child to two—or more.

The Big Rumpus: A Mother's Tales from the Trenches by Ayun Halliday. $15.95, 1-58005-071-9. Creator of the wildly popular zine *East Village Inky,* Halliday's words and line drawings describe the quirks and everyday travails of a young urban family, warts and all.

Breeder: Real-Life Stories from the New Generation of Mothers edited by Ariel Gore and Bee Lavender, foreword by Dan Savage. $16.00, 1-58005-051-4. From the editors of *Hip Mama,* this hilarious and heartrending compilation creates a space where Gen-X moms can dish, cry, scream and laugh. With its strength, humor and wisdom, *Breeder* will speak to every young mother, and anyone who wants a peek into the mind and spirit behind those bleary eyes.

Far From Home: Father-Daughter Travel Adventures edited by Wendy Knight. $16.95, 1-58005-105-7. Honest essays by both fathers and daughters offer inspiration and insight into how travel can affect this tender and complex relationship.

The Mother Trip: Hip Mama's Guide to Staying Sane in the Chaos of Motherhood by Ariel Gore. $14.95, 1-58005-029-8. In a book that is part self-help, part critique of the mommy myth, and part hip-mama handbook, Ariel Gore offers support to mothers who break the mold.

Whatever, Mom: Hip Mama's Guide to Raising a Teenager by Ariel Gore. $15.95, 1-58005-089-1. Hip Mama's back—dispensing wisdom, humor, and common sense to parents who've been dreading the big one-three (or counting the days until one-eight).